The Wilderness Detours

Course Corrections To Your Promise Land

Judah Lee Jacobs

"Seek correction to travel the right path, rather than inspiration for the wrong roads."

-Judah Lee Jacobs

Table of Contents:

Acknowledgements

This piece of work was by far the most rewarding project that I have taken part of in my entire life. I am extremely grateful for the Holy Spirit being my counselor, comforter, and teacher. I feel so blessed to have the awareness of God's grace and favor in my life. I have the utmost faith and hope that this book will change the lives of all those who choose to read it with soft hearts and "eyes that see and ears that hear" as the Lord teaches us. I was extremely careful this entire book to leave my opinion out of God's word and I can say proudly with unshaken integrity that the Holy Spirit is responsible and gets the glory for every letter written in this book.

I first would like to thank my wife, Shani Snow Jacobs, my very own gift from God, she is my everything. I have to acknowledge my family. My younger brother, for keeping me motivated to be the best and nothing less in everything I do. My five angels; my precious mother, she is my sunshine, my two sisters, and my grandmothers. I want to especially thank my father for guiding me to see and accept the truth in God's word. Because of him, I believe in my God-given identity, redemption, and that no power is greater than the power of our Lord and Savior, in which every knee shall bow. I also want to thank my father in law for teaching me about the comfort and peace that can be obtained through the Holy Spirit. Finally, I want to thank Pastor Anitha Jones of For His Glory Christian Fellowship for anointing me and bringing me up as a child in God's word. She has instilled in me perhaps two of the most important lessons that will always dictate the way I live my life. "This is my finest hour. I am blessed and I am dangerous because of God's ability." And lastly, "let everything we do in word and deed be FOR HIS GLORY!"

A PSALM OF SURRENDER

What do I have to do to feel your spirit and presence? What must I do to hear you? Faith comes by hearing, so speak to me. How can I get you to speak to me? I want to totally restart; I don't want to pick up where I left off. I want to restart our relationship. Talk to me as my Father, guide me. I don't know where to go. And I don't want to travel away from you. I repent. I feel that I have separated from you. Tell me all my flaws and sins. Tell me about my wrong motives. Please give me your motives. Please give me your will. Please let me feel you like the wind. Let me know my wrongs. Let me hear you clearly. Please talk to me. I am lost and want to hear your voice. You are my Shepherd, my King, and my Master Son of God. I am yours, I have strayed and I want you to bring me back to your flock. I am asking you to erase all my desires right now. Erase my desires, my wants, my goals, my dreams, and my opinions. Erase them completely. But write them back up as you wish. In my mind, write your desires, your wants, your

needs, your visions, and make your words my
opinion. I submit everything to you. To be your
soldier, I need a mission. Speak to me my God, The
Creator of Everything, the God of Enoch, Noah,
Abraham, Isaac, and Jacob. The God of David and
the Father of Yeshua my Salvation and King.
Forgive me and speak to me, faith comes by
hearing. And I want to hear you. Amen.

PHASE ONE: UNDERSTANDING THE WILDERNESS

"The wilderness is the beginning of you knowing The Father as Abba, which is the Hebrew equivalent of Dad and signifies your personal one on one relationship with Him as a child and servant."

Chapter: 1

WHAT IS THE WILDERNESS?

Something is missing. Uncertain smiles. Laughter is a distraction. Entertainment is therapy. The puzzle is incomplete. Searching for the meaning of life is so cliché. But the question still begs; why are we here? These are the thoughts of the **conscious** *mind. Something is missing. Uncertain smiles. Laughter is a distraction. Entertainment is therapy. The mind wanders while the body is anxious as we subconsciously search for the missing pieces to complete the puzzle. Aimless parties, drugs, alcohol, sex, television, sleep is romanticized or demonized. Aimless Living. For many,* **fulfillment** *is the missing link, while others continuously fall and fail trying to reach the concept of success society has created. Some of us have our own goals and visions that cannot seem to be grasped, no matter the wingspan of the work ethic. Either way we are trying to find middle ground or are stuck in the middle ground. The bible* *describes this middle ground as the wilderness. The place of travel for ideas to become visions and visions to become reality. The lack of understanding of God's wilderness is the reason we cannot get from A to B. If you don't know about God's wilderness, you don't know about your purpose.*

The wilderness is where God will take us before we begin our purpose. For many, the wilderness is where God will give us our purpose. Moses was over 80 years old when he received his purpose in the wilderness. He had a wife, kids, presumably, grandchildren. I'm sure he felt his life was complete or that his "best years" were behind him. However, in the wilderness God spoke to him and he learned that his life was just beginning. He received a new purpose and a new calling, greater than anything he could imagine. The wilderness has no regard for your age or your own presumptions on where you think your life is headed. When you enter God's wilderness he will often redefine, reinvent, and then redirect where he wants your life to go.

Why the wilderness? What is its significance? Is it literal? Spiritual?

Take a deep breath and relax. Don't think that I am asking you to grab a bug out bag, a camping tent, and machete to tough it out in your nearest forest for 40 days and nights. Although you certainly can, you don't have to. The word *midbar* is the Hebrew word for wilderness. It symbolizes anything from deserted, desolate, or isolated areas. The Israelites were considered to be in the wilderness because they were in a desolate area. They were *off the grid* if you may. This is essential in understanding God and receiving God's promises. Separating ourselves from the chaotic background noise and distractions in the daily grind allows us to hear His voice more clearly. For this reason and according to Luke 5:16, "Yeshua* often withdrew to the wilderness for prayer". Remember Romans 10.17, "…faith comes by hearing". Yeshua understood in order to hear God we have to know or recognize His voice because faith comes by hearing. We need to be certain of who is exactly speaking to us and become familiar with our Father's voice.

Jacob, Joseph, Moses, King David, John the Baptist, and Yeshua The Messiah* are arguably the six most important biblical people. Judaism would not exist at all without Jacob, Joseph, Moses, King David, and obviously Christianity would not exist without Judaism while John the Baptist and Yeshua The Messiah are the central figures in Christianity.

*Jesus Christ is referred to as Yeshua, his Hebrew name, to denote the meaning of His name, which means Salvation. Because along with being the Son of God, he is the Salvation of the world. The letter "J" is a relatively new letter as the Hebrew language does not have a phonetic sound for "J". Simply put "J" did not exist 2000 years ago in any language. It would have been impossible for his disciples or anyone else to call him Jesus. The name his mother Mary was commanded to name her son was Yeshua, and that is what he was called. For the purpose of study and to maximize learning from the ground up, the name Yeshua the Messiah will be used rather than Jesus Christ. *

These six key and essential figures in our faith share a common bond that is deeper than family relation and tribe. These Major Prophets that act as the backbone for the Judeo-Christian faith have all saved a generation from disaster in one way or another, but before doing so each and every one of them had to enter the wilderness at some point in order to be ready to perform their mission. The wilderness was mandatory for them. One way or another they all had to make a choice to enter their wilderness or be led to the wilderness by the Holy Spirit.

Beginning with Jacob, he was obedient to his father Isaac and instead of marrying a woman in the land of Canaan he made the journey back to Haran where his family was originally from to get his wife. It was Jacob's grandfather, Abraham, who received the promise that although he was a Hebrew living as a foreigner in the land of Canaan, his descendants would become numerous and conquer the land. It was in the wilderness where Jacob's journey began. In the wilderness, the Lord gave him his first vision and their personal covenant started on his journey to receive his promise. His name was later changed to Israel by God. 4,000 years later the descendants of Jacob and his nation still exist.

Joseph, one of the twelve sons of Jacob, and a patriarch of the people of Israel was sold to the Egyptians to be a slave in Egypt. After going through his many ups and downs, God was always with him and caused him to start from one of the lowest positions in Egypt to later becoming a Ruler of Egypt, second in command only to the Pharaoh. It was his status as a ruler of Egypt that preserved the life of his 11 brothers and his entire family through a harsh 7-year famine. Without him, the 12 tribes of Israel would not exist. But his journey started in the wilderness.

Moses had his first conversation with the Lord in the wilderness. It was there in the wilderness that he was instructed to be the leader that would deliver the Israelites from bondage.

King David was anointed by the prophet Samuel as a boy and defeated the giant Goliath when he was a teenager. But he dwelled in the wilderness as a fugitive and was 30 years old before becoming the second King of Israel.

John the Baptist lived in the wilderness his whole life before beginning his public ministry and introducing baptism to the world.

Finally, Yeshua the Messiah was led into the wilderness after being baptized by John and was tested in the wilderness for 40 days and nights before beginning his ministry which would ultimately save the world.

Hopefully, these people and what they accomplished are enough for us to examine the wilderness, and figure out why God leads those who are predestined to be great through the wilderness. All these people mentioned above were prophesied about before entering the wilderness. And as for those who consider themselves believers, the scriptures say in Jeremiah 1:5, *"I knew you before I formed you in your mother's womb. Before you were born I set you apart and appointed you…"* The Lord spoke these words to Jeremiah reminding him that he was called to be a prophet before he took his first breath.

The wilderness is a season of testing, development, isolation or transition. It can be a combination of any or all four depending on your calling. However, despite the specific calling, the wilderness is always a precursor for approaching promotion to a higher level or enhancing your relationship with the Holy Spirit. For some, they needed to be tested in order to build the necessary strength to succeed in that higher level. This was the case with Yeshua. Immediately after baptism he would begin his ministry which ultimately led to his death and crucifixion at stake, arguably the most inhumane and painful experience that humans have created. Yeshua had to prepare himself. That moment was always in the back of his mind and he always prayed for strength to endure it, it grieved him so much he shed tears of blood. For him, the wilderness was about preparation and prayer more so than anything.

For John the Baptist, the wilderness was about isolation in order to be holy enough and strong in the spirit to perform baptism on the Son of God. John grew up and lived in the wilderness, scriptures say he ate only honey and locusts. The wilderness for John the Baptist was about *preparation through separation.* And he was commanded to be a Nazirite from birth. The covenant of a Nazirite was all about extreme separation unto the Lord. A Nazirite was unable to even touch alcohol, wine, vinegar, raisins, grapes, nor anything from the grapevine, not even seeds or skins. This was to promote the utmost level of sobriety. During the course of the Nazirite vow, they could not go near a dead body, no matter the relation. Including father, mother, brother, or sister. If a person fell dead beside them the covenant was over. The hair of a Nazirite could not be cut during the entire vow and was a symbol of their separation of belonging to the Lord until the time of their covenant was over. Even just the slightest trimming of the hair was forbidden. The Nazirite vow in

Judaism is so rare and nearly obsolete in modern times because it requires a temple and animal sacrifices to finish the vow once it is complete. Generally, the vow was a few months to a few years because of the intense devotion and restrictions. However, in this day and age there is no temple to complete the vow, leaving a lifetime vow as the only option. No alcohol, vinegar, wine, fermented drinks, nothing from the grapevine, no funerals, a life of sobriety, and uncut hair makes the vow extremely difficult to keep for life. However, John was ordered to be a Nazirite from the womb until death. The wilderness for John the Baptist was the icing on the cake for him to be set apart and consecrated to the Lord in such a dramatic way to be qualified to be Elijah in the spirit and introduce baptisms to the world. This level of isolation and separation was how God ordained John the Baptist to be effective and prepared for His calling.

In the same way, the Israelites would be God's very own special people and their Kingdom of Israel would be God's Kingdom here on earth.

For the Israelites, the wilderness was about transition and preparation through separation to be ready to represent God in the Promise Land. In order for the Israelites to represent God, they needed to be distinguished. The wilderness is comparable to modern on-the-job training that most companies or businesses have today for their employees before they begin working independently without being shadowed or having to shadow. Every responsible company gives new hires an employee handbook and manual containing dress codes, employee conduct etc. based on the standards the company wishes to keep. In the wilderness, the Israelites received their personal employee handbook.

Now that we know the wilderness is mandatory, hopefully, we have decided that at one point or another we need to enter it. Let's take a closer look and examine what we might need and what happens in the wilderness, so we can pass through smoothly and enter our individual promise land that will connect us with our full potential.

The wilderness in the physical world is a very dangerous place. Many die in the wilderness today no matter the terrain, whether it is the mountains, jungle, desert, or even open waters. Increasing your chances of survival in the earthly wilderness requires serious preparation and an understanding of nature, navigation, and all threats present prior to journeying into the wild. In the same matter, but to an even greater extent, we need to be even more prepared before entering our spiritual wilderness. We need to understand what exactly we are getting ourselves into.

It is a must to look in the mirror and reflect on your most inner self. God's wilderness is a test that will reveal how far we are willing to go and how bad we want to live with a purpose and not just exist anymore but become alive in Him. If you truly want to wake up with a purpose for the rest of your life and be the best version of yourself, then the wilderness is mandatory. It is a must that you take the time to learn God's instructions for your personal journey and calling that He has prepared for you.

In the 1999 movie, The Matrix, actor Keanu Reeves played the role of Neo. In the Matrix, Neo is given an ultimatum of choosing the Blue Pill or the Red Pill. If he took the Blue Pill, he would continue to live in the synthesized, fictional, computer-generated world, in which he knew was not real. Or he could take the Red Pill and join the real world, unleashing his full potential, escaping the bondage of the fake world called the Matrix.

Many people claim and boast of having the knowledge that we as humans are more than flesh and bone, but spirits. It has almost become a trend to be spiritual and/or intellectual. Well, like Neo, a decision has to be made. If you know that you are more than flesh and bone and are ready to have a relationship with your Creator, The Creator. If you are interested in making God not just any god but YOUR God, if you want to know him by Name, Yahweh. Then you have to step into the wilderness.

Put an end to your bondage, the synthesized, artificial world and the way of thinking and living that accompanies that bondage. Enter the wilderness if you dare to know the will of God over your life and have the desire necessary to maximize your potential, and live out the promises that God has already declared for you.

The first step to entering this wilderness is to understand the bondage you are currently in. Pertaining to Israelites, they could only enter the wilderness after they decided to separate themselves from the bondage of being slaves in Egypt. Like the Israelites, you have to go through the wilderness in order to reach your Promised Land, except your wilderness is spiritual. And you will have to escape from what is keeping you in bondage, both physically and spiritually, which is not allowing you to be the best version of yourself. Before entering the wilderness, understand and identify the bondage in your life because your wilderness will be based upon the distance you can create between you and that bondage.

Chapter 2: LEAVING BONDAGE: YOU ARE RESPONSIBLE FOR YOUR OWN EXODUS

" YOU ARE A SLAVE TO WHAT CONTROLS YOU" -2 Peter 2:3

Before you think that you have gone through the wilderness or are in the wilderness and close to entering your promise land, understand that the wilderness, hardships, and tough times are all different. Do not confuse them. It is a very common misconception to confuse the wilderness with tough times or use the two concepts interchangeably. Be clear that tough times are not your wilderness. Israel experienced tough times in Egypt. The Israelites were in slavery before they entered the wilderness. Slavery. We can all agree that actual slavery is about as tough as tough times can get. But that was not their wilderness. In fact, the wilderness was so different and more challenging than slavery that many Israelites wanted to go back to slavery. But those were the Israelites who were not willing to go *through temporary adjustments to reach their full potential.* Although tough times, whether it be financial hardship, abuse, loneliness, tragedy, depression, loss of loved ones, marital problems, sickness, disease and other circumstances are difficult and overwhelming, many people are okay remaining in those situations because they are not willing to walk in the unknown, or step out on faith. Hence, the word bondage is what has you in chains preventing you from reaching your purpose, potential, promise land and all things related.

Although, we will experience the greatness of God in tough times and get to see God display his miracles. We still do not get to walk in half of our full potential while in bondage. We are delivered through tough times only when we are ready to step into the wilderness by leaving our bondage to be connected with our purpose and promises.

Just like the Israelites, we all have our own Pharaohs that keep us in bondage. Every day we wake up and robotically serve a system with full awareness that the system does not allow us to be whom we want to be, let alone who God wants us to be. We can find comfort in that system. Work. Eat. Sleep. Repeat. Work. Eat. Sleep. Repeat. There is comfort in security. But who are you working for and why? *Whose purpose are you living out? Who really reaps the benefits of your labor? Are you content with your work? And are you content with yourself?*

The systems that keep us in bondage are not always in the form of work. We can also be slaves to a culture. Being a slave to a culture can frequently be more dangerous than other forms of bondage, because the culture can control us subconsciously in every aspect of life, beyond our daily jobs. We will pay big money to be a slave to a culture. The symptoms of bondage tied to culture slavery are all mental. Certain cultures will dictate your opinion on what is right and wrong, and control your own senses to the point in which what is pleasure and pain are not even your own feelings or ideas. But instead a culture can construct the idea of pleasure and pain, and lead you to seek fulfillment according to the standards of what is trending, and conform your mind to match the concepts created by that culture. The common bond that all slaves to a culture share is a failure to ask the **"why's"**. *Why* did I spend so much on those shoes? *Why* am I wearing these clothes? *Why* do I have these aspirations? *Why* do I like or respect this person? *Why* do I care about culture "x" so much? The common bond of failure to ask the *why's* is just the precursor to the most dangerous and widespread problem among slaves to a culture; which is the **failure** to **care** about the *why's*. Meaning even if these questions arise to certain culture slaves, they just don't care about them. They don't see or have a problem with being a slave to a culture.

I have to break you out of this psychological slavery before guiding you through the wilderness. You cannot enter the wilderness until you truly from the bottom of your heart, identify your bondage and desperately want to regain control of the freedom and potential that God has waiting for you. This could require that you take a break and disconnect from people, interests, activities and hobbies that could be standing between you and God's purpose and plans for your life.

The Israelites reached a point in which they wanted to end their labor to the Pharaoh of Egypt and no longer serve his purpose. Instead, they wanted to fully serve God and live out their purpose and full potential. Which was to be a great nation and have their own kingdom rather than be slaves to another nation. In fact, they wanted this so bad that they shed tears for it.

"...The Israelites groaned in their slavery and cried out, and their cry for help because of their slavery went up to God. " Exodus 2:23

Israel's tears had finally reached the Lord and God had enough. Israel was ready to be delivered. And the Lord sent his prophet Moses to deliver them. Arguably, Moses most famous quote was, "let my people go!" Moses constantly told Pharaoh, "let my people go". But go where?

Pharaoh prevented the Israelites from worshipping God, which prevented the Israelites from being who they needed to be. Pharaoh was preventing the Israelites from living a life that reflected that of God's children, and special possession.

God has special and specific plans for those who are his children. We have to make it our desire to live the life our Father has waiting for us. Think about trust fund babies or children who are next in line to inherit their family business. They have jobs within the family company that are already theirs and waiting for them. They can make the choice to go into another line of work if they so choose. But in doing so, they will be missing out on what their parents have prepared for them. In the exact same way, God has an inheritance and Kingdom that is promised to his children. But when we choose to serve cultures, ideas and people separate from his Kingdom, we are voluntarily missing out on what our Father has prepared for us. We have no one to blame but ourselves. There is work for us to do within his Kingdom that requires his Holy Spirit to dwell inside of us. And the full power of the Holy Spirit cannot manifest itself in our lives if we are not devoted to living and working for God's Kingdom.

When we are ready to be who God has destined us to be, He will connect us with our deliverer. First and foremost, we need to be ready and willing to live out the Lord's promises instead of our own. He will deliver us. He will lead us into our wilderness and promise land. But we need to be sick, tired and fed up with our bondage. We need to be sick and tired of the culture that leads us astray from God's calling. We need to be sick and tired of being sick and tired. Making sure our tears reach the Lord must be top priority.

So many tears are shed in vain and many prayers seemingly go unheard because we cry in vain, we pray in vain. We pray without purpose. Sometimes as much as we claim we are done with being in bondage, the Lord knows our hearts. He knows if we had the opportunity to leave, WE WOULD STAY PUT WITH OUR PHARAOHS. We cannot lie to the Lord, he knows our hearts. We often times claim to be about a certain lifestyle, but we're not. We love to pretend that we are fed up with our circumstances, but we're not. The most difficult thing about tough times is that we frequently have to adapt in order to survive and maintain some level of peace and sanity. But what happens in that process is we get comfortable once we adapt. We can become comfortable with the people who treat us the worse. We can get comfortable at the job we hate performing. We can get comfortable in our bad habits that hurt our loved ones, not to mention ourselves. We adapt to what pains us and causes sorrow. The survival instinct of adapting works against us in tough times. Becoming comfortable during tough times through adapting to survive is what paralyzes us on our journey to reaching and walking in our full potential.

Making the choice to no longer endure the environment, people, and circumstances we hate to be involved with will bring us a step closer to our promise land. But we need to be done accepting the small and few perks of bondage. Yes, all bondage has its perks. The abusive relationship can provide shelter, the robotic job provides consistent paychecks, the drugs and substances numb the pain. Bad friends, provide good laughs. Only if we are truly ready to step out and away from those perks and circumstances will God connect us with a deliverer.

REFLECTION QUESTIONS:

Who are the people in your life that you consistently want out of your life that you consistently keep in your life?

If any, what are the benefits and consequences of keeping these people around in the short and long-term future?

What are your "every day" negative behaviors and habits you choose not to give up on?

If any, what are the short and long-term benefits of these behaviors and habits? What are the short and long term consequences of these behaviors and habits?

Develop a list of *why's* that you can ask yourself about your daily walk. Literally examine all paths and decisions you make every day, from the people you talk to, the route you drive or walk to work or to class, the stores you shop at, and your social media life.

The *why's* frequently point to the intentions behind our decisions which can lead us to discover what cultures or people can subconsciously have control over us.

We need to figure out the benefit and gain we get from these people, behaviors, cultures and habits so that we can supplement them with positive; people, behavior, habits, and purposeful cultures. It is necessary to know these factors in order to make it through the wilderness. But first, make sure that you are actually fed up and ready to put your bondage behind you. The level of being fed up needs to reach a point of tears, anger and frustration if we expect intervention on God's behalf. Think of Eric Thomas the "Hip Hop Preacher" and his famous saying, "When you want to be successful as bad as you want to breathe, then you'll be successful". We need to be fed up with what keeps us in bondage to the point where it is heart-breaking.

Chapter 3: Solve Your Identity Crisis By Establishing Belief in Your God Given Identity:

"Who you think you are will determine what you accept and don't accept in life"

WHO ARE YOU?

Gaining your **true** identity takes place in the wilderness. The first 5 books of the Bible are called Torah in Judaism. In Hebrew, Torah means the *Instruction,* and is derived from the Hebrew word *yarah,* which means *"hit the mark"*. For this reason Apostle Paul defines sin as "missing the mark". The mark he is referring to is the Torah. Genesis, Exodus, Leviticus, Numbers, and Deuteronomy are the English translations of the Hebrew titles of the first 5 books of the Bible. What the books mean in Hebrew is *"In The Beginning"* (Genesis), *"God gave us names"* (Exodus), and *"Spoke to Us"* (Leviticus), *"In the Wilderness"* (Numbers), *"His Words"* (Deuteronomy). The sixth book is the book of Joshua where the Israelites reach their Promise Land. Through the order of the Torah (Book Of

Instructions), we learn the plan that God has laid out before we can reach our Promised Land and how "to hit the mark".

If you are looking for God's identity over your life, you are going to have to be a **man** or a **woman** of God first. That is at **the forefront** of every important biblical person's mind. They worshipped and praised, the Father, which is why they got out of bed in the morning. The rest of their identity stemmed from their fellowship with God, and while many of us claim to be believers, we only pray in times of need. We only ask for the things that we want. From now on, we have to make ourselves prayer warriors above all else. We need to be in communication with God every single day. God heard the Israelites through their crying out and prayers. God can no longer be 'just God' to you. He has to be *your* God.

The movie *300* is the story of the courageous Spartan warriors from Ancient Greece. The Spartans chose to go to battle with only 300 men. In one scene, King Leonidas, played by actor Gerard Butler and his Spartans were approached by an allied Arcadian army who wished to join forces. The Arcadian leader told King Leonidas that his Arcadians brought more soldiers, because he noticed the Spartans only had 300 soldiers. But King Leonidas asked the Arcadian soldiers what their daytime profession was. One by one they replied, "sculptor, poet, craftsman." Then he asked his Spartan's soldiers, "What is your profession?" With a unanimous battle cry, his 300 Spartans responded, "AAUU! AAUUU!" King Leonidas then corrected the Arcadian leader and said, "I brought more soldiers".

He was saying "we are not full-time chefs or poets who can also wield a sword when duty calls. But we are just Spartans, just soldiers. We do not live to cook and then if the time comes to fight we are down for that too. We are Spartans, we live to fight, and when the time comes to cook, we cook." The Spartans were and still are world renowned for their dedication to combat. Some of their combat formations and strategies are used today, nearly 2500 years later. They did not train for battle, they lived for battle.

In the exact same way, when you become a man or woman of God you are making the decision to become a disciple. For a disciple, prayer is not just a coping mechanism in times of stress. Prayer and obedience to God need to be at the center of your joy and daily routines. Everything else will flow from your discipleship. Being a disciple is about being the best possible student and believer of Yeshua you can be. And a disciple then creates other students of Yeshua. Make the decision to become a 24/7, 365 disciple and center your life around being a knowledgeable disciple and producing knowledgeable disciples. Most importantly, your joy needs to come from this relationship with God and what you do to maintain it. When that becomes your identity, the plans God has already established over your life will be made clear to you as you go through the wilderness of dedicating yourself to the Lord by separation.

In order for you to believe in yourself, you have to know exactly who you are. This is why being a disciple is so critical. Nothing can happen in your life spiritually until you believe in your identity, until you believe in what you learn. Believing in what you have learned is what will enable you to apply that knowledge. When the Lord puts a calling over your life he will give you a brand new identity or remind you of your predestined identify as he did with Jeremiah. Sometimes he does this literally with a name change just as he did with Joshua, Israel's first leader and even Israel himself whose was once Jacob. Moses means to be "drawn out". Reiterating once more, Moses, lived 80 years before he knew and walked the identity that God gave him. The wilderness is where Moses discovered that it would be his responsibility to draw his people out of slavery.

Your identity is not just about your name, but it has everything to do with the purpose you serve. This is why the Israelites cried out for their slavery to end, they believed they were not slaves and refused to accept those circumstances. They prayed for their slavery to END, not get better. That bondage we spoke of earlier is only accepted because of no knowledge of self. The Israelites believed in the God of their ancestors and believed in the identity that God gave to their ancestors.

Once we make this decision to believe in God and our God-given identity, "he will give us the desires of our hearts". However, that *does not always* mean our current desires but that means he will give us what he wants us to desire. For many of us, the thought of exchanging our current goals or dreams does not sound appealing. Let's just be honest. Some dreams we may have had since childhood. Some goals are passions that we are willing to die for. The very thought of living without those passions is not appealing. We have to be honest. However, when you embrace being a child of God and he happens to put something new on your spirit; submit to that desire. Often times his desire and vision for our life is bigger, better, more meaningful, and always more eternal than we can imagine. Be willing to explore and surrender to his desires rather than your own. When you decide to pray, read and understand scripture in the wilderness, the Holy Spirit will speak to you, but it will be your responsibility to respond back. Once we yield to the Holy Spirit the desires of our heart will be renewed.

Examine the first wilderness experience of Moses. God first spoke to Moses through a burning bush. It was only when Moses decided to respond back to God, that he learned about his identity. Moses could have run away, or could have thought to himself, " I must be crazy". In fact, he should have thought he was crazy. But he didn't. He entertained the idea that it was really God speaking to him. He chose to fully commit to that conversation. He could have walked away at any moment. But on the inside he wanted purpose. God gave Moses a purpose and plan for his people that was bigger than Moses could have ever imagined. God needed Moses to be the deliverer of the Israelites and lead them from slavery to the Promise

Land. This was such an incredible calling. When the Lord spoke to Moses, he gave Moses and the Israelites a greater calling than they could have ever imagined.

Think about this, the Israelites were slaves in Egypt for centuries. I'm sure as slaves they always had dreams of being free. They once lived in Egypt peacefully without being slaves. I'm confident that it would have been appealing for the Israelites to return to being the minority in Egypt without the oppression and cruelty of slavery. Moses did not have to say "let my people go" so we can leave Egypt. He could have fought for civil rights in Egypt and the Egyptians and Israelites could have formed one kingdom and just received better treatment. That would have been ideal. The Israelites had no land of their own, they were slaves for centuries.

Similar to the blacks living in America today, the Israelites could have just blended and been like the now African Americans. The Israelites

could have just been called the Egyptian- Israelis.
But that was not the desire God put over the
Israelites. In fact, it was God that commanded
Moses to tell Pharaoh, "let my people go".

Consider that the Africans Americans living
in America are no longer slaves; they fought for
civil rights and are now active members and leaders
in the country they were once enslaved in. African
Americans were slaves for 400 years in America.
150 years after the end of their slavery, some can
argue they still face racism; they are for a fact the
minority.

The Israelites were in the exact same
situation. Slaves for 400 years. But God gave them
their own land. They were no longer the minority.
The head and not the tail. This is the difference
between God's thinking and what I call "accessible
planning". I will elaborate on "accessible planning"
later. Allow God to steer your minds, and exchange
your plans for His plans for often times his plans are
greater.

Like Moses, you will have the opportunity to speak to God in the wilderness. Except it will be His Holy Spirit speaking. Your burning bush will be God's Word and when you read it will be your responsibility to become receptive to God's word and listen and speak back to the Holy Spirit. This may sound crazy but Moses was faced with the same decision, and he turned out alright. Once you become obsessed with God, He will become obsessed with you. The more He is on your mind, the more you will be on His Mind.

"In the beginning the Word already existed.
The Word was with God,
and the Word was God.
He existed in the beginning with God.
God created everything through him,
and nothing was created except through him.
The Word gave life to everything that was
created,"

- John 1

Reflection Questions:

Are you ready to leave behind what others want you to be?

Are you ready to be who God wants you to be at the expense of saying goodbye to your dreams, visions, goals?

Would you trade yours goals for his goals?

If you are willing to make these compromises for yourself then you are ready to enter the wilderness. Your identity and your belief in that identity is what will keep you grounded when the going gets tough and obstacles come your way.

PHASE 2: THE WRONG ROADS

"Fear and negativity or courage and positivity have everything to do with the perception of how we view obstacles"

This second phase is dedicated to examining the wilderness experience of the Israelites, who had the roughest experience of all people in the Bible that traveled through God's wilderness. Through studying their ups and downs, we can learn from their mistakes in order to travel more efficiently in our own wilderness. The wilderness experience of the Israelites will serve as our blue-print and road map, as the trials they faced are mandatory for every wilderness experience. During the examination of the Israelites wilderness, New Testament parallels will be mentioned to highlight and hammer in key concepts of the wilderness experience.

Chapter 4: FOLLOWING GOD WILL ALWAYS BE DEFIANT: WOULD YOU FOLLOW GOD?

*"The Lord hardened the heart of Pharaoh, and he **chased** after the Israelites who left with **their fist raised in defiance."** – Exodus 14:8*

Many of us try to walk on two separate paths because of our inability to let go of the past. The end result is failure to fully commit to any path. We cannot follow through with what is good or bad for us. C students in all walks of life. **Full potential requires full commitment**. This concept holds true in relationships, finances, school, work, and even health. Making the choice to not let go of people, substances, and habits that hinder us from reaching our full potential is the sure fire way to self-sabotage the journey to the promise land. You have to make the decision to follow and pursue what you want relentlessly without looking back.

When we track the Israelites journey from Egypt to the wilderness, they were initially being chased. There are people that are depending on you to stay with them in bondage. When you make the decision to follow God, is when those against your purpose will try and keep you from it. The moment you follow God will also be a very revealing moment for those who claim to be on your side.

In the book of Exodus, the Pharaoh agreed to let the Israelites go peacefully but he changed his mind once they left. This inevitably will always happen like clockwork. When you attempt to send yourself in a positive direction, negativity always follows to keep you off track. This is like the "crabs in a barrel" analogy. Always remember there are people in your life depending on you for their ego boost, or for their own good times, and even depending on you to serve them. There are thousands of husbands, and boyfriends that simply won't eat if their wife or girlfriend doesn't cook. People can be dependent on you in many ways both positive and negative. Whether or not that is a problem comes down to personal preference, but it can and will become a personal problem for you when these people interfere with you being the person that God has called you to be. Nothing comes before that.

"God first", right? Everyone says that but nobody wants to live it. We all know people who promise never ending support and they swear loyalty until the end. Once you walk with the Lord and follow him by putting Him first, you have to immediately open your eyes and be aware of whom or what will chase you. What you may discover is that you could potentially be your own worst enemy. Those old habits and behaviors that crippled you from success in the past will be right next to those old friends and on the list of new foes that want to keep you in bondage. On the bright side, those who are loyal to you will remain loyal and walk with you. But those who are not will attempt to pull you back into the bondage that you were crying to get out of.

It's up to you to choose the people and habits that board your ship to success. What you allow and don't allow to exist on your ship will dictate whether you sink or sail smoothly. Although modern thinking has its perks, the idea of *coexistence* does not always work.

Two opposing goals **cannot** *coexist*, something has got to give. The Israelites wanted to be their own nation, with their own land, and not be slaves. But Pharaoh wanted the Israelites to be slaves to Egypt and serve him in Egypt. Unfortunately for Pharaoh, the Israelites made the decision to let him down. We need to be aware of potential Pharaohs that will try to drag us back into bondage. For many of us, our old self will act as a Pharaoh and we will need to run from the desires, and ideas that our old self has in order to reach the promise land and become the new person we want to be. Don't expect to be a new person while keeping your old mind, because the priorities of the old mind will become obstacles for the new mind, hindering the opportunity for you to have new priorities. Without new priorities, you will be stuck in the same position wasting away wondering why your window of opportunity was never opened.

The idea of opposing goals being unable to coexist is spoken of frequently by Yeshua in the New Testament. Yeshua issues a warning to those who wish to follow him, *"If you want to be my disciple, you must hate everyone else by comparison--your father and mother, wife and children, brothers and sisters--yes, even your own life. Otherwise, you cannot be my disciple."* This is a very hard message to receive, but he needed people to understand that if you choose to follow him, there is no turning back. One reason is because bridges will be burned. But more importantly he is giving a warning that the goals and desires of everyone else must come second to his. He was a man on a mission; he had so much he needed to accomplish in so little time. And he needed his disciples and followers to be on the exact same page with his mission.

You have to have the same attitude as Yeshua in regard to people you keep around you. If they don't have your mission, then their mission can potentially interfere with yours and they cannot share the same path with you.

Again Yeshua says, *"Whoever wants to be my disciple must deny themselves and take up their cross daily and follow me."* These are hard messages to accept, but if you believe that you are not flesh and bone, but spirits, then you must be ready to live for the spirit. And the work of God requires his disciples not to live for themselves, but live for his will. Not for the will of the flesh.

These are examples of conversations Yeshua had with people who wished to be his disciples but were not qualified.

"He said to another man, 'Follow me.' But he replied, 'Lord, first let me go and bury my father.' Jesus said to him, 'Let the dead bury their own dead, but you go and proclaim the kingdom of God.' Still another said, 'I will follow you, Lord;

but first let me go back and say goodbye to my family.' Jesus replied, 'No one who puts a hand to the plough and looks back is fit for service in the kingdom of God.' –Luke 9:59-62

Very hardcore and radical, but these people who were unfit to follow Yeshua would not have made it in the Israelite's wilderness either. Think back to the Israelites leaving Egypt, there was no turning back once they stepped into the wilderness. For any reason, going back to Egypt would not have worked out. In both the old and new testament, we are looking at the same story with different people. The disciples that chose to follow Yeshua were on the same mission as the Israelites seeking their Promised Land.

The disciple Matthew, worked at the Tax Office and Yeshua walked in and told him to come with him. Scriptures say plainly that, Matthew, *"got up, left everything and followed him."* Believing in who God is and trusting him allows this to happen. The Israelites believed in the God of their ancestors, and the disciples believed Yeshua was the Messiah. Here are other examples of the defiant and immediate nature in which other disciples began to follow Yeshua.

"As Jesus was walking beside the Sea of Galilee, he saw two brothers, Simon called Peter and his brother Andrew. They were casting a net into the lake, for they were fishermen. "Come, follow me," Jesus said, "and I will send you out to fish for people." 20 At once they left their nets and followed him." – Matthew 4:20

"...he saw two other brothers, James son of Zebedee and his brother John. They were in a boat with their father Zebedee, preparing their nets. Jesus called them, and immediately they left the boat and their father and followed him." – Matthew 4:21-22

This type of strong faith with action can only happen when you trust God more than yourself. Trusting that you would rather have God in control of your life than yourself. Believing you're better off serving him and working for him rather than anyone else comes down to trust. John 6:29 says, the work of God is this…. "To believe in the whom he sent". When you believe in Yeshua and the Father, you believe that they are in control. Make the decision to do the work of God and Yeshua rather than anybody else's work and rather than your own. Trust that their work will give you fulfillment.

CHAPTER 5: THE ILLUSION OF BEING TRAPPED

"They are to encamp by the sea… Pharaoh will think, 'The Israelites are wandering around the land in confusion, hemmed in by the desert.' And I will harden Pharaoh's heart, and he will pursue them. But I will gain glory for myself through Pharaoh and all his army, and the Egyptians will know that I am the LORD."

Exodus 14:1-4

After the Passover was established, the Israelites were spared by the angel that came and killed all the firstborn in Egypt. Pharaoh then agreed to let the Israelites leave, but only to immediately pursue them. The Lord caused the Pharaoh to chase the Israelites so that his glory could be displayed.

When we enter the wilderness and decide to follow and obey God, we will have the appearance of being defeated to those who chase us. The appearance of defeat is a matter of physical perception rather than spiritual perception. Pharaoh made this mistake with the Israelites as did Satan with Yeshua. Sometimes this is what God wants. He needs us to be completely broken so that we can be completely dependent on his Holy Spirit and Him. Once we rely on God and His Holy Spirit we will see our circumstances through a spiritual scope, and our confidence will be renewed.

The Lord took the Israelites to a specific position where they were cornered and surrounded by the Egyptians. The only way out was through the sea, but the Israelites had no boats. This sense of being corned spread fear throughout the Israelite camp. There will be a time in the wilderness where we have to resist the urge to be afraid and panic despite the appearance of what could be an obstacle.

Our only responsibility will be to trust in God and remain calm in these cornering circumstances. This was the first time in the wilderness that the Israelites became afraid and they began to doubt if they should have ever left bondage. The Israelites allowed panic to overwhelm them, causing thoughts of defeat and they complained to Moses.

"Was it because there were no graves in Egypt that you brought us to the desert to die? What have you done to us by bringing us out of Egypt? 12 Didn't we say to you in Egypt, 'Leave us alone; let us serve the Egyptians'? It would have been better for us to serve the Egyptians than to die in the desert!"

13 Moses answered the people, "Do not be afraid.
Stand firm and you will see the deliverance the
LORD will bring you today. The Egyptians you see
today you will never see again. 14 The LORD will
fight for you; you need only to be still." Exodus 14

The Israelites fear had everything to do with perception. Through their own lenses they thought themselves to be surrounded with nowhere to run. Fear and negativity or courage and positivity have everything to do with the perception of how we view obstacles. When we enter the wilderness we force God to be responsible for our lives and well-being. That is the beauty of voluntarily entering the wilderness. We will always arrive at a place where at first, second, and even a third glance we appear to be trapped. Choosing to depend on God will always be our best bet.

Allowing yourself to depend on God is difficult because in doing so, we lose our *"sense of power"* and ability to control a situation. I say *" sense of power"* because it generally is an **illusion** of control that we believe ourselves to have. But replacing God's control with your own will lead you out of these cornering circumstances.

You have the freedom to try to be in control of your life and destiny, but **remember your own power does not have the ability to part seas.** When the Israelites surrendered to God, they no longer had to run. God parted the sea and the Israelites walked across. Relying on God is not just an opportunity to see and experience his miracles, but it will save you from wasted movement on your journey.

Coming full circle, remember that the miracle of parting the sea only took place because the Israelites camped where God told them to. **Obedience** and *following* God put them in a situation to experience his miracles. Obedience to God can give you the assurance that you are on the right path.

How many times have we created stress in our lives because of the dozens of options we have? Choosing the right road is often a difficult choice.

This comes from being the dictator and "calling the shots" in your life. Allow God to call the shots by becoming obedient to His word and you will soon find the clear way out of overwhelming circumstances.

Reflection Questions:

Are you ever anywhere you are not supposed to be?

Could being in the wrong place be taking you out of position for advancement to your purpose?

CHAPTER 6: THE IMPATIENT PATH: SHORTCUTS TO SHORTCOMINGS

"Impatience will be one the first obstacles to overcome in the wilderness, but making God's schedule your schedule is the crushing blow that defeats impatience."

Understand it is not an overnight process to reach your full potential or accomplish your goals. God has a process of preparing you to be who he needs you to be by the time you reach your goals, in order to represent him the best you can according to his will. This was a very difficult concept for the Israelites to understand. The Israelites had a very rough transition from slavery to their Promised Land because they couldn't grasp God's concept of preparing you for your next level **before** you're able to walk in it. The Israelites were in the wilderness for 40 years and it should have been an 11 day journey. A biblical understanding of the wilderness will prevent you from making the same mistakes as the Israelites.

Before the Israelites could even leave for the wilderness, God's first order of business was establishing the Passover and Festival of Unleavened bread. Before any other laws were given and before any details were described with how to perform any rituals, or ceremonies, God changed the calendar of His people.

"The Lord said to Moses and Aaron in Egypt, "This month is to be for you the first month, the first month of your year" Exodus:12:1

God is serious about setting his people apart from everyone else. Being set apart is the essence of being holy. Seriously think about this, he said the month of March* (Abib *Nisan in Hebrew) was going to be when they bring in the new year. The calendar change is symbolic of God saying you are no longer operating on your time or anybody else's time, but you are operating on God's time. This is why the 7th day Sabbath is given well and long before the 10 commandments and other laws. The Israelites had to operate on God's time in order to perform the Passover ritual and be spared of the disaster that would come across Egypt. When you are in cooperation with God's time both in and out of the wilderness, you can also be saved from disaster and become distinguished in His sight

This reminds me of being a teenager and getting myself into trouble because I operated on my time rather than my mother's. Her time would have kept me from being arrested and many troubles I found myself in simply because I was out too late. God sets the same rule HE WILL NOT

ALLOW you to travel with him until you embrace the concept of his time and his calendar rather than your own. This will save you from mistakes that accompany operating on your own schedule.

Remember that God will prepare you for these obstacles if you have taken heed to his instructions before entering. Establishing His calendar for your life, will prepare you to handle the temptation of being impatient.

Immediately after the Israelites received the 10 commandments, the first thing the Israelites did was break one of them. The urge Israelites have to be impatient was because they made a public announcement of entering the promise land and a triumphant exit from bondage. And they felt as if all eyes were on them.

This happens all the time in our lives; we make these public announcements and update everyone about our next big moves, job opportunity, or relationship status. Sometimes for good reason, and sometimes for bad. But now all eyes are on us. And all we want is for our announcements to come to pass. The Israelites were camped in *seemingly* the same position for too long and grew impatient.

"...the people saw that Moses was so long in coming down from the mountain, they gathered around Aaron and said, "Come, make us gods who will go before us. As for this fellow Moses who brought us up out of Egypt, we don't know what has happened to him."

In the wilderness, Moses frequently went up to the mountain to pray and speak to God. Meanwhile, while he was finishing receiving the rest of the laws and commandments. The Israelites grew tired in waiting for Moses and assumed he was dead. So they took it upon themselves to appoint a new leader and came up with what seemed like a brilliant idea to create an altar of gold they melted into the shape of a calf. There are a million different lessons to learn from this one story so let's go through a few.

Because of Moses age, the Israelites assumed he was dead. Seems reasonable, he was over 80 years old and hiking up and down a mountain. After not being seen for 40 days, they came up with the conclusion that he died and even convinced his own brother of it. They were eager to keep on making progress in the wilderness and grew tired in waiting.

When other people are aware of your goals, sometimes with good intentions they try to help you. In this case, the Israelites suggested incorrect counsel to Aaron, Moses' brother. Not waiting on the Lord will cause you to feel behind in what it is you are trying to accomplish. This is why operating on God's calendar is so crucial. The Israelites violated the commandment of idolatry they were just given and it stemmed from the fact that they were impatient.

The Israelites needed to know God's commandments and laws and put them into practice in the wilderness, so they could have the laws mastered and understood by the time they reached the Promised Land. Although the Israelites believed they were ready to advance, they only received the 10 commandments. Moses had a whole book to give them. Remember Yeshua says, *"The student who is fully trained will become like the teacher"*. The Israelites were not fully trained, and could not yet become like the teacher.

While they were eager to continue making progress, they were not ready. You have to remember that in your wilderness God is developing you to be ready for your purpose and your Promise Land to *represent* Him. You have to trust God with the progress and time frame for advancement in your life. When feeling the urge to make decisions based on time constraints, assess if you have all the information needed to move forward. The Israelites did not have the information needed to advance and they proved they had not yet mastered the information they just learned.

"You shall not make for yourself an image in the form of anything in heaven above or on the earth beneath or in the waters below. You shall not bow down to them or worship them; for I, the LORD your God, am a jealous God, punishing the children for the sin of the parents to the third and fourth generation of those who hate me, but showing love to a thousand generations of those who love me and keep my commandments"
Exodus 20:4-5

The only reason idolatry happened was because of impatience. When you become impatient you will try to force progress and be creative to your own demise. FOCUS ON THIS! The Israelites **did not INTEND** on worshipping the gold calf, they were worshipping God. The calf was simply an alter to worship God. But the impatience and leaving God's plan for their own plan meant they had to rely on their own thinking and strategy rather than God's thinking and strategy. In the process of depending on their own thinking, they forgot about God's laws. Usually, straying from God's Laws happens when we think with our own logic rather than HIS logic. His logic is found in scripture. When you read scripture you will gain an understanding of His logic. If we look to his laws we will get his answers, and his plans.

In this situation, not one of the Israelites involved checked with God's law before making a decision. So while in and out of the wilderness we have to be weary of whom we have as counsel and whom we associate with that can influence our decisions. Only receive advice from those who make decisions based off God's laws. The first King of Israel named Saul made the same mistake. *".... Saul saw the vast Philistine army, he became frantic with fear. He asked the LORD what he should do, but the LORD refused to answer him, either by dreams or by sacred lots or by the prophets. Saul then said to his advisers, "Find a woman who is a medium, so I can go and ask her what to do."*

His advisers replied, "There is a medium at Endor." -1 Samuel 28:5-7

The reason why there was no medium was because when Saul was doing his job well as king of Israel, he ordered all the mediums out of the land. His advisors knew that already. His advisors should have never allowed him to consult a medium. This mistake was one of the many that led to Saul's death. So although we have to be aware of our foes in the wilderness, it is more important to be aware of the type of people we have in our circle that we consider friends. Their perspective on your progress can alter your decisions, and their advice can redirect your journey to your promises.

The temptation to be impatient in the wilderness is one of many that Satan will use to derail your journey to your purpose. Your wilderness is spiritual, and Satan will always offer a physical solution to a spiritual problem. And the underlying factor in all of Satan's temptations will be less time and less endurance for immediate benefits. Every gift and calling the Lord gives his children is spiritual but can be used physically. Satan's trick is to lure you by showing you an abundance of physical rewards to trade in your spiritual calling for a physical gain. Satan attempted to try this type of bargain with Yeshua in the wilderness.

He wanted Yeshua to trade being the King of the everlasting world for King of the non-eternal physical world. Had Yeshua accepted Satan's offer he would no longer have to suffer a death at stake or wait to be crowned King. However, Yeshua knew that according to what the Prophets wrote before him, that it would be his ability to endure a painful death and resurrection that would make him worthy to be crowned King, and make the world righteous because of his sacrifice. Yeshua was thinking long term and eternally while Satan was thinking short term and was concerned about what was perishing.

"...the LORD's good plan will prosper in his hands.
When he sees all that is accomplished by his anguish,
 he will be satisfied.
And because of his experience,

my righteous servant will make it possible
for many to be counted righteous,
  for he will bear all their sins.
I will give him the honors of a victorious soldier,
  because he exposed himself to death.
He was counted among the rebels.
  He bore the sins of many and interceded for
rebels."

Prophet Isaiah 53: 10-12

Yeshua chose to be a "Kingdom Thinker", he chose to be patient and endure the struggle to be made worthy of being crowned King. He chose to endure death only to bare the sins of mankind, so mankind can have the opportunity to be counted righteous. He refused to take the non-painful, non-enduring easy route for a temporary run in office in the always fading, soon to be ending physical world.

God grants eternal blessings to those who patiently endure for the sake of His Kingdom. If you are willing to go through the physical pain and humiliation to be knocked down by the world, you will be stood back up and exalted by God.

Reflection Questions:

What are the mountains in your life that require endurance for the climb?

Do not try climbing *any* mountain just to say you have climbed one. Instead, look for *THE Mountain* that you are supposed to climb and never exchange *The* Mountain for any mountain because of unwillingness to endure.

Your mountain and your identity go hand in hand, do not be tempted by the spirit of impatience that allows you to settle for any mountain or a lesser mountain. Stay true to the endurance required for your mountain.

CHAPTER 7: MERGING LEFT ON SATISFACTION

".... personal satisfaction is the fork in the road heading the opposite direction of self control"

"The grave and destruction can never be full, so the eyes of man can never be satisfied." Proverbs 27:20

King Solomon explains in proverbs that satisfaction is a part of our nature. But understanding both sides of the proverb, is that waiting on the other side of satisfaction is death and destruction. Not exercising self-control in that aspect of our human nature will allow the always hungry Death and Destruction (known as Sheol and Abaddon) to consume you. In this proverb, Death and Destruction are personified as looking to fill their chambers with people who allow their eyes to seek satisfaction. Sheol and Abaddon are mentioned in the Bible as the Grave and Bottomless Pit. Seeking satisfaction at the wrong times will put you or your dreams on a detour to these destinations.

You have to make a choice and be strong and dependent on the Spirit to overcome satisfaction just as Yeshua did when Satan tried to tempt him in the wilderness.

"...Jesus led aside of the Spirit into the wilderness, to be tempted of the devil. And when he had fasted forty days, and forty nights, he was afterward hungry. Then came to him the tempter, and said, if thou be the Son of God, command that these stones be made bread. But he answering, said, it is written, Man shall not live by bread only, but by every word that proceedeth out of the mouth of God." Matthew 4:1

Yeshua being most knowledgeable was well aware of what happens when you first enter the wilderness, so he skipped the mystery and took it upon himself to fast. He was ready to be unsatisfied. His knowledge and preparedness is why his wilderness experience is summed up in just eleven verses. Whereas, the Israelites is nearly four entire books.

"If only the LORD had killed us back in Egypt," they moaned. "There we sat around pots filled with meat and ate all the bread we wanted. But now you have brought us into this wilderness to starve us all to death."Exodus 16:3

Finding satisfaction in the wilderness will not happen and should not happen. Satisfaction leads to complacency and God would never want you to be complacent before reaching your promise land. It's pointless. Satisfaction and complacency will cause you to dial down on your work ethic and maybe even faith. God knew beforehand the Israelites would be in actual battle soon enough. Therefore, sitting comfortably with a full stomach in the wilderness is not a good idea.

We all can relate to the pleasures of enjoying our favorite piece of cake, succulent lobster, juicy steak, or any other favorite dish. When we indulge on these pleasures they give us a temporary euphoria and complete satisfaction, but only during the moment. And delicious food can often be a remedy to reducing stress. However, this will take your eyes off the prize. Getting full too soon will leave no room for dessert.

God wants us to avoid complacency in the wilderness because the wilderness is not our final destination, but a means to arrive at our final destination fully equipped to be a champion when we get there. When we seek satisfaction in the wilderness we fall into one of the Israelites first major mistakes.

Complaint after complaint against God and Moses drove the Israelites in the wrong direction. Similar to being impatient seeking satisfaction opens the door to other problems that will take you off course.

"Then the foreign rabble who were traveling with the Israelites began to crave the good things of Egypt. And the people of Israel also began to complain. "Oh, for some meat!" they exclaimed. 5 "We remember the fish we used to eat for free in Egypt. And we had all the cucumbers,

melons, leeks, onions, and garlic we wanted. *⁶ But now our appetites are gone. All we ever see is this manna!" Numbers 11:4-8*

Overlooking the blessings in your current circumstances will always lead to reminiscing on the past rather than the future. But more importantly it will cause mistakes in the present. Instead of Israel looking at the manna as the miraculous blessing that it was, they chose to see it as lack of variety in their diet. The Israelites grew tired of the manna that literally came from heaven. This only happens when we forget about why were in the wilderness, or when we lose sight of our purpose. Seeking satisfaction at the wrong times will lead to **boredom** and eventually cause straying away from where you need to be. Overlooking their current blessings caused the Israelites to think back to bondage. Remember earlier what I said about how we can experience perks in our tough times that keep us from leaving.

There will come a time in the wilderness when the few things we enjoyed in our bondage will entice us. But by staying focused on the promises ahead by being appreciative of the blessings in the now, we can overcome that enticement. All the Israelites needed to do, was think about the expense of the fish they thought was "free". Notice how in the scriptures it was the foreigners who mentioned the free fish and old things of Egypt. They were not all slaves like the Israelites were.

Immediately the Israelites should have recognized that the foreigners did not have their same struggle in Egypt. This is why we have to surround ourselves with people who have an equal or stronger drive and work ethic. Hanging around people who do not want success as much as you will drive you in the wrong direction. Especially, in times when mental strength is necessary. Nothing was free for the Israelites in slavery. For a slave to think something is free is an oxymoron in and of itself. These foreigners caused the Israelites to deceive themselves. Just like you lie and deceive yourself when you find every reason in the book to stay in that unhealthy relationship, or to keep your addiction going. The Israelites were lying to themselves.

We do the same thing. We lie about our careers all the time. We pretend that we are well paid; we put on a fake smile every day, have fake friendships with our coworkers, and act like our boss would never fire us. That was how Israel was thinking. They pretended like everything was "all cool" back in Egypt. Take heed. DO NOT be the slave that thinks he eats for free! Everything in your bondage comes at a cost. In the wilderness, Satan will try to use this same trick against you. In order to be ready for this deception, we have to be honest about the lies in our life so that we do not deceive ourselves.

The Lord eventually sent the Israelites meat and lots of it, but the Israelites gorged on the meat and made God angry.

"...the people went out and caught quail all that day and throughout the night and all the next day, too. No one gathered less than fifty bushels! They spread the quail all around the camp to dry.[33] But while they were gorging themselves on the meat—while it was still in their mouths—the anger of the LORD blazed against the people, and he struck them with a severe plague. [34] So that place was called Kibroth-hattaavah (which means "graves of gluttony") because there they buried the people who had craved meat from Egypt."

Eventually the Israelites got what they wanted, but only to their own demise. This story always reminds me of people with shopping addictions, whether for food, clothes or any items that can be purchased in bulk. How many times have you been in a store and promised yourself you would only buy one item, but left with several bags and drained your bank account? We make these mistakes all the time with finances and food. Our eyes become bigger than our bellies. Although we take our eyes being bigger than our bellies lightly, God calls it glutton and greed and nothing is funny about it to him.

Making a practice of greed and glutton spirals into the dependence of your joy shifting from God to a new addiction. Addictions come in the form of anything that becomes habitual at the expense of harm to yourself. Remember the wilderness is our training ground or classroom. We have to be attentive to what we can be learning in all circumstances, because that knowledge will have to be applied later.

For example, the promise land some of us are seeking to arrive in will lead to lucrative financial gain and advancement. If we are not prepared to handle having a prosperous amount of money, food, and status in the wilderness then it will lead to our destruction when we are out of the wilderness. Managing the pleasures God gives us without being greedy, proves that our head is above the clouds and things below don't have control over our joy. Not handling wealth or abundance of what should have been a blessing will lead you to the same fate as these greedy Israelites.

And for any modern Christians that think the "Old Testament" God has no mercy and the "New Testament" God is merciful and the message is all Love, you are greatly misinformed. God is the same then, now, and is never changing. He is merciful and loving in the "Old Testament" as well as the "New Testament. Yeshua warns us to avoid greed in order to save us from the same fate as the Israelites that succumbed to being gluttonous.

"...if you are untrustworthy about worldly wealth, who will trust you with the true riches of heaven?" Luke 16:11

Yeshua teaches this when two rich men ask how to get to heaven. One is willing to give up half of his possessions and he receives the Kingdom, while the other is not.

"...a man came running up to him, knelt down, and asked, "Good Teacher, what must I do to inherit eternal life?"

18 "Why do you call me good?" Jesus asked. "Only God is truly good. 19 But to answer your question, you know the commandments: 'You must not murder. You must not commit adultery. You must not steal. You must not testify falsely. You must not cheat anyone. Honor your father and mother.'[e]"

20 "Teacher," the man replied, "I've obeyed all these commandments since I was young."

21 Looking at the man, Jesus felt genuine love for him. "There is still one thing you haven't done," he told him. "Go and sell all your possessions and give the money to the poor, and you will have treasure in heaven. Then come, follow me."

22 At this the man's face fell, and he went away sad, for he had many possessions."

If you consider yourself godly and have plans on making money in the future, then learn from the Israelites mistake. Once you prove to God that you can handle prosperity without greed, he will allow you to move forward in the wilderness. Looking to splurge and feast will keep you at a standstill; IF God is directing your plans. Consider it a favor if you are greedy with "a real big spender" mindset and never reach the goals that will allow you to be "a real big spender". Trust me; God is looking out for you.

Once God knows that you can handle your position of wealth, he will allow you to move forward because you will be a blessing to others and the poor. In the wilderness, be on your guard to prove to yourself and show the Lord that you are ready to handle and receive the blessings that could potentially be waiting for you. Think of the man Zacchaeus who gained Salvation for his entire home, because of what he was willing to give for the sake of Yeshua and to inherit the Kingdom of God.

"Jesus came by, he looked up at Zacchaeus and called him by name. "Zacchaeus!" he said. "Quick, come down! I must be a guest in your home today."

Zacchaeus quickly climbed down and took Jesus to his house in great excitement and joy. But the people were displeased. "He has gone to be the guest of a notorious sinner," they grumbled.

Meanwhile, Zacchaeus stood before the Lord and said, "I will give half my wealth to the poor, Lord, and if I have cheated people on their taxes, I will give them back four times as much!"

Jesus responded, "Salvation has come to this home today, for this man has shown himself to be a true son of Abraham. For the Son of Man came to seek and save those who are lost."

Luke 19:2-10

If you are not ready to be Zacchaeus, then pray for development in this area of your life. What you will discover is that there is still doubt wavering somewhere in your mind about the Kingdom of God, or lack of understanding. God is trying to prepare us to think eternally rather than just about the moment. The desire to store up wealth here on earth is to gain security and comfort. Our whole lives are devoted to securing a reliable pension or retirement, so we can kick back and relax. It is the considered the wise thing to do, and in fact it is. However, securing our eternal lives and eternal homes in His Kingdom should take precedence over securing temporary comfort while on earth. Yeshua teaches a parable of the foolish rich man.

"A rich man had a fertile farm that produced fine crops. [17] He said to himself, 'What should I do? I don't have room for all my crops.' [18] Then he said, 'I know! I'll tear down my barns and build bigger ones. Then I'll have room enough to store all my wheat and other goods. [19] And I'll sit back and say to myself, "My friend, you have enough stored away for years to come. Now take it easy! Eat, drink, and be merry!"'

²⁰ "But God said to him, 'You fool! You will die this very night. Then who will get everything you worked for?'"

²¹ "Yes, a person is a fool to store up earthly wealth but not have a rich relationship with God." Luke 12: 13-21

Yet another person to fall victim to satisfaction. If this man applied the instructions of the Torah, he would have prioritized his life differently. But in order to apply this wisdom and instruction of the Torah we have to do soul searching and ask ourselves if we truly believe in it. Belief will lead to knowledge, and applying it will save us from making these mistakes. But if you don't apply the knowledge you learn in the Torah then you will share the fate of others who also didn't apply the knowledge.

If you are a believer who questions the current validity of the Old Testament and Torah, then don't take my word for it, but take the words of Yeshua. Yeshua warns ahead that there will be a time that people will fall into the trap of distancing themselves from the Torah. Below is an interesting translation of Matthew 24 taken from the Complete Jewish Bible, Yeshua specifically warns of people not applying the Torah, or first 5 books of the Holy Bible.

"At that time many will be trapped into betraying and hating each other,[11] many false prophets will appear and fool many people; [12] and many people's love will grow cold because of increased distance from Torah. [13] But whoever holds out till the end will be delivered." Matthew 24:10-14 Complete Jewish Bible

Another prophecy of Yeshua that has already proved itself to be true. Many today are divided on the legitimacy and application of the Torah in modern times. And some pastors and teachers lead people astray by aiding their listeners in not applying it to our daily lives. But do not rely on your pastor for your own salvation. At this point we can clearly see that the Torah lays out the steps for inheriting our Promise Land and reaching his

Kingdom, which is our true Promise Land, the New Jerusalem that is spoken of in the Book Of Revelation. So take it upon yourselves, not your pastor to read, believe, and understand the Torah or Book of Instructions. For good measure and to hammer in this idea, here are a few more teachings from lips of Yeshua advocating the Torah that Moses gave to the Israelites.

"There was a certain rich man who was splendidly clothed in purple and fine linen and who lived each day in luxury. [20] At his gate lay a poor man named Lazarus who was covered with sores. [21] As Lazarus lay there longing for scraps from the rich man's table, the dogs would come and lick his open sores.

[22] "Finally, the poor man died and was carried by the angels to be with Abraham.[a] The rich man also died and was buried, [23] and his soul went to the place of the dead.[b] There, in torment, he saw Abraham in the far distance with Lazarus at his side.

²⁴ *"The rich man shouted, 'Father Abraham, have some pity! Send Lazarus over here to dip the tip of his finger in water and cool my tongue. I am in anguish in these flames.'*

²⁵ *"But Abraham said to him, 'Son, remember that during your lifetime you had everything you wanted, and Lazarus had nothing. So now he is here being comforted, and you are in anguish.* ²⁶ *And besides, there is a great chasm separating us. No one can cross over to you from here, and no one can cross over to us from there.'*

²⁷ *"Then the rich man said, 'Please, Father Abraham, at least send him to my father's home.* ²⁸ *For I have five brothers, and I want him to warn them so they don't end up in this place of torment.'*

²⁹ *"But Abraham said, 'Moses and the prophets have warned them. Your brothers can read what they wrote.'*

[30] *"The rich man replied, 'No, Father Abraham! But if someone is sent to them from the dead, then they will repent of their sins and turn to God.'*

[31] *"But Abraham said, 'If they won't listen to Moses and the prophets, they won't be persuaded even if someone rises from the dead.'" Luke 16: 19-31*

"Don't misunderstand why I have come. I did not come to abolish the Law of Moses or the writings of the prophets. No, I came to accomplish their purpose.[18] *I tell you the truth, until heaven and earth disappear, not even the smallest detail of God's law will disappear until its purpose is achieved.* [19] *So if you ignore the least commandment and teach others to do the same, you will be called the least in the Kingdom of Heaven. But anyone who obeys God's laws and teaches them will be called great in the Kingdom of Heaven.*

[20] *"But I warn you—unless your righteousness is better than the righteousness of the teachers of*

religious law and the Pharisees, you will never enter the Kingdom of Heaven!"

Matthew 5:17

"Not everyone who calls out to me, 'Lord! Lord!' will enter the Kingdom of Heaven. Only those who actually do the will of my Father in heaven will enter.²² On judgment day many will say to me, 'Lord! Lord! We prophesied in your name and cast out demons in your name and performed many miracles in your name.' ²³ But I will reply, 'I never knew you. Get away from me, you who break God's laws.'"

Matthew 7:21

CHAPTER 8: DOUBT IS THE HIGHWAY OF DISOBEDIENCE: MOSES PROHIBITED FROM THE PROMISE LAND

"Doubt is the reliance on past experiences that shuts the door on new opportunities."

MOSES THE DELIVERER OF THE ISRAELITES! THE PROPHET OF GOD! Moses raised his staff to part the seas! Moses gave the Law of God to Israel! Moses and God spoke as friends do, face to face. God showed Moses his glory on Mt. Sinai. God gave Moses the task and responsibility to deliver Israel from bondage in Egypt to the Promise Land. Moses was *The Man*! Now that you're all excited about Moses, let me remind you that Moses the Great prophet died in the wilderness. He did not reach the promise land. Let that sink in. Moses, the friend of God. Leader of Israelites. Moses bar none is the most highly esteemed prophet 2nd to Yeshua in all scripture. He talked to God face to face. God personally came from his throne and introduced himself to Moses and walked with Him. Not an angel, not an archangel, not the Holy Spirit, but God himself.

If you think your goals are destined and guaranteed and that nothing will stop you, you have been greatly misinformed. It's great to have confidence. You have to believe in yourself and who you are supposed to be. But in order to help you I have to first give you some humble pie. You ain't Moses.

I want you to understand that even the great prophet Moses was forbidden to enter the Promised Land because he chose to be disobedient to God's instructions.

"You and Aaron must take the staff and assemble the entire community. As the people watch, speak to the rock over there, and it will pour out its water. You will provide enough water from the rock to satisfy the whole community and their livestock."

⁹ So Moses did as he was told. He took the staff from the place where it was kept before the LORD. ¹⁰ Then he and Aaron summoned the people to come and gather at the rock. "Listen, you rebels!" he shouted. "Must we bring you water from this rock?" ¹¹ Then Moses raised his hand and struck the rock twice with the staff, and water gushed out. So the entire community and their livestock drank their fill."

¹² But the LORD said to Moses and Aaron, "Because you did not trust me enough to demonstrate my holiness to the people of Israel, you will not lead them into the land I am giving them!" Numbers: 20

This story confuses many people and raises a lot of eyebrows. The most common question is what did Moses and Aaron do wrong? Why did he strike the rock? The miracle still happened, what difference did it make? Take a close look at how God told Moses to speak to the rock rather than strike the rock. This was the second time that Moses had to perform a miracle of getting water from the rock. The first time Moses had to strike the rock.

"Walk out in front of the people. Take your staff, the one you used when you struck the water of the Nile, and call some of the elders of Israel to join you. ⁶ I will stand before you on the rock at Mount Sinai.[b] Strike the rock, and water will come gushing out. Then the people will be able to drink." So Moses struck the rock as he was told, and water gushed out as the elders looked on. "
Exodus 17

Notice how in Numbers 20, God tells Moses to *speak* to the rock rather than *strike* the rock with his staff. As we see in Exodus which was when the Israelites first entered the wilderness and even in Egypt, Moses only used his staff to perform miracles. So when God asked him to speak to the rock, Moses had to believe it would work without his staff. Say hello to **doubt.**

Doubt caused Moses to put limitations on what was possible. Do not let your past best performances dictate the way you go about your future goals. Notice that God told Moses and Aaron that they did not **trust** him. The **doubt** in the miracle is what led to their disobedience.

When we choose to be disobedient to God it is because we choose to doubt rather than trust. We make the decision to give into certain desires because we believe that we won't be content unless those desires are fed. Understand that giving into the desires of certain sin, is all about doubting the feeling of contentment unless you give way to the sin.

This happens for people who set fitness or health goals but are never able to reach them. In my collegiate track career, I was a sprinter and did martial arts. My peers always looked to me for fitness advice or health questions. Everyone is initially always so serious about trying to get into shape. The hardest part is always the diet. People would ask me, "how do you have a six pack, how can I get muscles, or lose weight, and what should I eat and avoid eating?" They ask for my strategies. My response is the same no matter what.

As far as diet, I don't eat any dairy or red meat, and I stay away from fried foods. Like clockwork; man, woman, or child, they all say with an equal level of passion and confusion, "NO DAIRY! What do you mean by no dairy? What about my cereal? And I love cheese! No cheese?" I always promise results of getting leaner just by eliminating the dairy, but very few people are willing to even try it out.

They are not open to dropping the dairy and believe they will never be content or completely satisfied without cheese on their turkey burger. Although *they don't try it*, they don't *believe* me, they **doubt** that their diets will bring the same **satisfaction** now that dairy is missing. Doubt is the reliance on past experiences that shuts the door on new opportunities.

God wanted Moses to speak to the rock to display another level of His holiness and power to the people of Israel. Did Moses ever stop to think that it was not the staff performing the works but God? Moses struck the rock twice out of anger, which visually can take God out of it. Had Moses spoke to the rock it would have been an even greater miracle and God's presence and power would have been evermore clear to the people that Moses was his prophet of choice.

Believe that God's instructions and laws are enough for you to be who God has called you to be. Doubt will prevent you from being better than your past. Moses would have no longer needed the staff. He was going to reach a new level of being a prophet of God. Be careful to follow the instructions of the Lord, because disobedience to those instructions can hinder you from stepping into your purpose.

Chapter 9: The Israelites Detour

" At some point in the wilderness, the rubber has to meet the road"

For most of us the likelihood of God asking us to strike a rock for water will not happen. God did not require the rest of the Israelites to perform any miracles, nonetheless they still needed to hold no doubt of what God can do.

The Promise Land for the Israelites was described as the land flowing with milk and honey, an abundant land with all the resources available for every single one of the Israelites to live prosperously. All the Israelites needed to do, was take it over from the current residents of the land who were seen as wicked in God's sight. As the Israelites were nearing the end of the wilderness, God commanded they send 12 spies to scout the land of Canaan and give back a report for the rest of Israel.

"Send out men to explore the land of Canaan, the land I am giving to the Israelites." Numbers 13:2

The 12 spies went into Canaan for 40 days and nights and came back with a report for the Israelites. Initially, they had an excellent report and their spirits were high. The Israelites learned that no exaggeration was given regarding the abundance of the land. They carried back a grapevine from the land that required two men just to hold it.

God wanted Israel to get a glimpse that their wilderness experience was worth it. He was showing them that all the separation and trials would finally pay off and that they would be the generation of Israelites to bring in the blessing that was promised to them nearly 700 years before they were born. The Israelites had their dreams within arm's reach.

The bad news was that 10 of the 12 scouts were frightened by the people of land. The little fear that they spoke of was enough to scare all of Israel.

"But the people living there are powerful, and their towns are large and fortified. We even saw giants there, the descendants of Anak! …. We

can't go up against them! They are stronger than we are!" So they spread this bad report about the land among the Israelites: "The land we traveled through and explored will devour anyone who goes to live there. All the people we saw were huge. [33] We even saw giants[b] there, the descendants of Anak. Next to them we felt like grasshoppers, and that's what they thought, too!"

Numbers 13:28-33

Are you the person that allows a small amount of negativity to always outweigh the positive? The Israelites focused on what would be at best a tough temporary battle for the land, instead of thinking about the generations after them that would inherit this abundant land. This fear opened the door for the Israelites to doubt their God. The Lord had already punished Moses for his doubt and now the Israelites were next. Their doubt once more led to complaining and the reminiscing on bondage. Doubting always comes from unbelief, there is no other explanation. Doubting means you don't fully believe. The option to have doubt will always be present. But treat doubt like an enemy and fight it, go to war against doubt by walking out what God requires you to believe. God awards those who chose to live without doubt but instead rely on the Lord's strength. But he punishes those who choose to walk down the road of doubt.

"...The whole community began weeping aloud, and they cried all night.[2] Their voices rose in a great chorus of protest against Moses and Aaron. "If only we had died in Egypt, or even here in the wilderness!" they complained.[3] "Why is the LORD taking us to this country only to have us die in battle? Our wives and our little ones will be carried off as plunder! Wouldn't it be better for us to return to Egypt?"[4] Then they plotted among themselves, "Let's choose a new leader and go back to Egypt!"

God responds "....as surely as I live, and as surely as the earth is filled with the LORD's glory,[22] not one of these people will ever enter that land. They have all seen my glorious presence and the miraculous signs I performed both in Egypt and in the wilderness, but again and again they have tested me by refusing to listen to my voice. ²³ They will never even see the land I swore to give their ancestors. None of those who have treated me with contempt will ever see it. ²⁴ But my servant Caleb has a different attitude than the others have. He has remained loyal to me, so I will bring him into the land he explored. His descendants will possess their full share of that land. ²⁵ Now turn around, and don't go on toward the land where the Amalekites and Canaanites live. Tomorrow you must set out for the wilderness in the direction of the Red Sea.[b]"

²⁶ Then the LORD said to Moses and Aaron, ²⁷ "How long must I put up with this wicked community and its complaints about me? Yes, I have heard the complaints the Israelites are making against me. ²⁸ Now tell them this: 'As surely as I live, declares the LORD, I will do to you the very things I heard you say. ²⁹ You will all drop dead in this wilderness! Because you complained against me, every one of you who is twenty years old or older and was included in the registration will die. ³⁰ You will not enter and occupy the land I swore to give you. The only exceptions will be Caleb son of Jephunneh and Joshua son of Nun.

³¹ "'You said your children would be carried off as plunder. Well, I will bring them safely into the land, and they will enjoy what you have despised. ³² But as for you, you will drop dead in this wilderness. ³³ And your children will be like shepherds, wandering in the wilderness for forty years. In this way, they will pay for your faithlessness until the last of you lies dead in the wilderness.

³⁴ "'Because your men explored the land for forty days, you must wander in the wilderness for forty years—a year for each day, suffering the consequences of your sins. Then you will discover what it is like to have me for an enemy.' ³⁵ I, the LORD, have spoken! I will certainly do these things to every member of the community who has conspired against me. They will be destroyed here

in this wilderness, and here they will die!"
Numbers 14

The wilderness that should have been their stronghold turned into their tomb. Faithlessness will make you stuck in the place of transition. The wilderness was never supposed to be the last stop. There will come a time in your wilderness in which the rubber has to meet the road. The Israelites backed down and out of that moment, making them unworthy to be the generation that would represent God in the Promise Land, in his Kingdom.

God expects all of his children to live boldly; a proverb of King Solomon says that *"the godly are as bold as lions".* And in the book of Revelation cowards are grouped with the people who will not inherit the Kingdom of God. Never forget the Lord is the same and never changing.

"I am the Alpha and the Omega, the Beginning, and the End. I will give off the fountain of the water of life freely to him who thirsts. He who overcomes shall inherit all things,

and I will be his God and he shall be My son. But the <u>cowardly, unbelieving</u>, abominable, murderers, sexually immoral, sorcerers, idolaters, and all liars shall have their part in the lake which burns with fire and brimstone, which is the second death."
Revelation 21: 6-8 KJV

PHASE 3: THE WOLVES IN SHEEPS CLOTHING THAT DEVOUR DREAMS

Branching away from the mistakes of the Israelites, other groups of people in the Bible missed out on their inheritance based on a few wrong turns that later proved to put them on a road parallel to the promised land, but the separate paths would never intersect.

CHAPTER 10: ACCESSIBLE PLANNING: LAZINESS, AND FEAR:

"Accessible planning is settling for less, because of the unwillingness to put in the work for what is beyond arm's reach."

The first person in the Bible to miss out on their inheritance and promise was Esau, Jacob's older brother. The nation of Israel should be Esau's nation because the eldest brother is entitled to receive the father's will ahead of the younger brother. Many believe that Jacob took the birthright and inheritance from Esau because of trickery. The first instance was when Esau was starving and Jacob offered him a meal for the birth right. The second instance was when their mother Rebekah devised a plan for Jacob to pretend to be Esau when Isaac their father gave his son's their final blessing. This was certainly not the case. Esau missed out on his birthright long before Jacob received it.

The name Jacob in Hebrew is Yaakov, which means to supplant or replace. Supplant does not mean to steal, but rather dethrone. This does not have to be by force, but by out strategizing or outworking another person to obtain what you want for yourself. Jacob was willing to work harder than Esau for his descendants to inherit what was promised to their grandfather Abraham.

God made a promise to Abraham that although he and his wife Sarah lived as foreigners in the land of Canaan, they would one day own the land and be as numerous as the stars in the sky. The key here is that God was going to make these two and few foreigners and minorities of the land become the majority. This is why Abraham's son Isaac married Rebekah who was also a foreigner to Canaan and a Hebrew. She was from Haran, the same place Abraham and his wife Sarah were from. Isaac and Rebekah lived in Canaan as two foreigners and minorities just as Abraham and Sarah. However, their eldest son Esau did not marry women from Haran, as was the custom. He decided to marry two young women from Canaan where they were living at the time. Very big mistake! Not only were these women rude to his mother Rebekah, any children produced from these women would not be in line to receive Abraham's promise. Just as Ishmael, Abraham's son from the Egyptian women Hagar could not receive the promise.

However, Jacob remaining obedient to his father Isaac chose to enter the wilderness at his father's command and journey to Haran to get his wife Rachel. Not to mention Jacob worked 14 years for Rachel's father to earn her as his wife. After the 14 years, Jacob took all of his family back to Canaan. The difference between Jacob and Esau is laziness, obedience and hard work. Jacob was willing to do anything he could and be obedient in order to receive God's promises. He wanted to be special to God, and in return his descendants known as the Israelites are considered God's very own special people and possession. This was only possible because of the depths Jacob was willing to travel in order receive the blessing and have that relationship with God.

Meanwhile, Esau did what was accessible. From an early age, he proved that his inheritance was worth a single meal. And he was not willing to make the journey like Jacob to get a wife from their homeland. Esau was **not** willing to enter the **wilderness**. Esau's goals were a product of *tunnel vision*. He was only willing to work for what was in plain sight, and grasp what was within arm's reach.

On the other hand, Jacob chose to "walk by faith and not by sight". He set out on a journey into the unknown and received his vision from God, which was well beyond his wildest dreams. But his trust in God, work ethic, and willingness to enter the wilderness to receive his grandfather's blessing is why his descendants are still known 4000 years later.

CHAPTER 11: COVENANTS: DRIVING IN THE HOV LANE

"He that walketh with the wise shall be wise: but a companion of fools shall be afflicted. "

Proverbs 13:20

The second person to miss out on a promise is Jacobs's eldest son Reuben. The Messiah should descend from the tribe of Reuben, but instead Yeshua the Messiah comes from the fourth eldest son Judah's tribe, which is the leading tribe in Israel. Judah is not the leading tribe because of anything particular or special he did, rather it is the particular mistakes of his 3 older brothers that cost them their birthrights. The sexual lust of Reuben with his father's wife made him disqualified for the inheritance. These are the final words Jacob spoke to his son Reuben.

"Reuben, you are my firstborn, my strength,
  the child of my vigorous youth.
  You are first in rank and first in power.
But you are as unruly as a flood,

and you will be first no longer.
For you went to bed with my wife;
 you defiled my marriage couch.

Genesis 49: 3-4

"Your are first no longer." Imagine if these were the last words your father spoke to you. It was Jacob's responsibility to prophesy over his children according to the will of God. Being a man of God, Jacob had very much forgiven Reuben. Just like God our father will forgive us when we sin and repent. However, in this case, although Reuben was forgiven it did not mean he would still be first among his brothers.

His sin and poor decision was more than violating his father, Reuben slept with one of his brothers mothers, violating his brothers as well. This more than likely changed a dynamic of trust between him and the men in his family. He proved himself untrustworthy. How can you be a leader to people that don't trust you?

Reuben's sin has less to do with sex and everything to do with the people we choose to make covenants and contracts with. Reuben's number one priority should have been his securing his inheritance and being a leader as the eldest of 12 siblings. But his sexual agreement with his father's wife conflicted with his goals. This begs the question of what was his father's wife thinking?

If his father's wife really had Reuben's best interest in mind she would not have slept with him. Not to mention remaining loyal to her husband. We need to assess the relationships we are in covenant or contracts with from sexual, marriage, friendships, and even work and business relationships. Assess the purpose of all these relationships and the goals in these relationships.

Prisons across America and the world are filled with individuals who for whatever reason became in covenant with the wrong people. Your personal covenants can rule you out from receiving God's promises just like Reuben.

Even in marriage it was the godly woman Abigail who had the wicked and foolish husband that was going to get her family and all the male servants killed. But Abigail chose what was right over her covenant in order to help King David because he was God's anointed King. Your covenants, contracts, and relationships will either be a blessing or a curse for you. There is no in-between. In the case of Abigail and her husband Nabal, she had to choose between what was best for the greater good in God's Kingdom or her own covenant with her wicked husband Nabal.

"...one of Nabal's servants went to Abigail and told her, "David sent messengers from the wilderness to greet our master, but he screamed insults at them. 15 These men have been very good to us, and we never suffered any harm from them. Nothing was stolen from us the whole time they were with us.16 In fact, day and night they were like a wall of protection to us and the sheep.17 You need to know this and figure out what to do, for there is going to be trouble for our master and his

whole family. He's so ill-tempered that no one can even talk to him!" -1 Samuel 25:14"

Nabal, Abigail's first husband lacked *godly intelligence*. His thoughts, directions and decisions he chose to walk in relied on his way of thinking which was foolish. He rejected looking after David and his soldiers and chose not to return a favor for David. Everyone in Israel and Judah knew that David would be King, that he defeated Goliath, and that he was anointed by the Prophet Samuel. David was respected in all of Israel and Judah. Nabal's refusal to lend a hand to David went against what was best for the entire Kingdom of Israel.

Saul was the king that everyone wanted out of office, and he was in pursuit of David to kill him. David had to flee to the wilderness to escape from Saul's grasp. David and his men were living the wilderness as fugitives at the time. But David would be King over Israel as this was what the people wanted. Even Saul's own men wanted David to be King. Nabal knowing this should have taken the opportunity when he had the chance to aid the Kingdom of Israel by assisting King David, God's anointed King.

You and everyone in your circle should make decisions that are based on what is best for God's kingdom, family, loved ones, and the greater good. Nabal lacked the necessary leadership and it lead to the endangerment of his household, all because he was not thinking about God's Kingdom. He was not a *Kingdom Thinker*.

Meanwhile, Abigail had the spiritual intelligence to understand God's way and how to put her knowledge of God's way into practice. The knowledge you attain is irrelevant unless it can be applied. Abigail was *a Kingdom Thinker*, and she was considered a wise woman of God throughout scripture. We all need to strive and pray to have the courage to be like this godly woman Abigail. She eventually went out herself and spoke to King David just before King David and his men were coming to kill Nabal and all his male servants.

Pay close attention to how the story unwinds…

Abigail wasted no time. She quickly gathered 200 loaves of bread, two wineskins full of wine, five sheep that had been slaughtered, nearly a bushel[b] of roasted grain, 100 clusters of raisins, and 200 fig cakes. She packed them on donkeys [19] and said to her servants, "Go on ahead. I will follow you shortly." But she didn't tell her husband Nabal what she was doing….

"Abigail, said to David, "I accept all blame in this matter, my lord. Please listen to what I have to say. [25] I know Nabal is a wicked and ill-tempered man; please don't pay any attention to him. He is a fool, just as his name suggests.[d] But I never even saw the young men you sent.

[26] "Now, my lord, as surely as the LORD lives and you yourself live, since the LORD has kept you from murdering and taking vengeance into your own hands, let all your enemies and those who try to harm you be as cursed as Nabal is. [27] And here

is a present that I, your servant, have brought to you and your young men. ²⁸ Please forgive me if I have offended you in any way. The LORD will surely reward you with a lasting dynasty, for you are fighting the LORD's battles. And you have not done wrong throughout your entire life.

²⁹ "Even when you are chased by those who seek to kill you, your life is safe in the care of the LORD your God, secure in his treasure pouch! But the lives of your enemies will disappear like stones shot from a sling! ³⁰ When the LORD has done all he promised and has made you the leader of Israel, ³¹ don't let this be a blemish on your record. Then your conscience won't have to bear the staggering burden of needless bloodshed and vengeance. And when the LORD has done these great things for you, please remember me, your servant!"

³² David replied to Abigail, "Praise the LORD, the God of Israel, who has sent you to meet me today! ³³ Thank God for your good sense! Bless you for keeping me from murder and from carrying out vengeance with my own hands. ³⁴ For I swear by the LORD, the God of Israel, who has kept me from hurting you, that if you had not hurried out to meet me, not one of Nabal's men would still be alive tomorrow morning." ³⁵ Then David accepted her present and told her, "Return home in peace. I have heard what you said. We will not kill your husband."

³⁶ When Abigail arrived home, she found that Nabal was throwing a big party and was celebrating like a king. He was very drunk, so she didn't tell him anything about her meeting with David until dawn the next day. ³⁷ In the morning when Nabal was sober, his wife told him what had happened. As a result, he had a stroke[e] and he lay paralyzed on his bed like a stone. ³⁸ About ten days later, the LORD struck him, and he died.

David Marries Abigail

³⁹ When David heard that Nabal was dead, he said, "Praise the LORD, who has avenged the insult I received from Nabal and has kept me from doing it myself. Nabal has received the punishment for his sin." Then David sent messengers to Abigail to ask her to become his wife.

40 When the messengers arrived at Carmel, they told Abigail, "David has sent us to take you back to marry him."

41 She bowed low to the ground and responded, "I, your servant, would be happy to marry David. I would even be willing to become a slave, washing the feet of his servants!" 42 Quickly getting ready, she took along five of her servant girls as attendants, mounted her donkey, and went with David's messengers. And so she became his wife. – 1 Samuel 18-42

The bible is so amazing in its prophetic nature and foreshadowing of events. This story is set to serve as an example for us believers today to follow the steps of Abigail. When we decide to imitate Abigail and forsake what is evil in order to serve God and be a servant to King David, we find ourselves being called into a marriage covenant with the very one who sits on King David's throne. King Yeshua, from the royal line of King David.

3,000 years later you have the same choice as Abigail. You can carry on in covenants that you know are foolish. And you can remain in those covenants to the demise of your well-being along with the well-being of those around you. Or you can become a Kingdom Thinker and serve the very one who sits on King David's Throne.

CHAPTER 12: ANGER AND UNFORGIVENESS: SIMEON AND LEVI

"Anger is the smoke that clouds your vision in times when godly perception is required."

"Simeon and Levi are two of a kind;
   their weapons are instruments of violence.
⁶ May I never join in their meetings;
   may I never be a party to their plans.
For in their anger they murdered men,
   and they crippled oxen just for sport.
⁷ A curse on their anger, for it is fierce;
a curse on their wrath, for it is cruel.
I will scatter them among the descendants of Jacob;
   I will disperse them throughout Israel."

Genesis 49:5-8

Now that Reuben was unfit to lead the 12 tribes, Simeon and Levi were next in line to be leaders and receive their fathers blessing.

Unfortunately, Simeon and Levi missed out on their full potential and God's promises because of a few lifestyle choices that reflected deeper aspects of their character.

Simeon and Levi's thinking was clouded by anger, and the path that seemed right in a single moment was their major mistake. The 12 brothers had 1 sister named Dinah, who was obviously very dear to them. Tragically and horrifically Dinah was raped by a prince named Hamor from a neighboring town. God agreed that this prince had greatly defiled, wronged and violated Dinah. Long story short, in an act of revenge, Simeon and Levi devised a scheme and killed the prince along with *every* single male in the town.

"...Simeon and Levi, who were Dinah's full brothers, took their swords and entered the town without opposition. Then they slaughtered every male there, including Hamor and his son Shechem. They killed them with their swords, then

took Dinah from Shechem's house and returned to their camp." Genesis 34:25-26

If you think that was a bit excessive, Jacob felt the same way. It would have been justifiable if they only killed Prince Hamor. But why the whole town? They were lead by their anger.

Your anger will lead you to temptation and steer your decision making. Anger is the smoke that clouds your vision in times when godly perception is required. Not being in control of your anger will take you out of the position God needs you to be in. Anger will inspire you to make permanent decisions based off temporary emotions.

"...don't sin by letting anger control you." Don't let the sun go down while you are still angry, for anger gives a foothold to the devil." Ephesians 4:26-27

This scripture is not saying don't be angry. For anger is a regular human emotion, we should get angry, not often by any means. Anger can come from being passionate about something. What we are obliged to do, however, is control our anger and not allow that anger to be with us all day. Scriptures say, "be slow to become angry". Madness and anger can rush us, but we have to literally fight the urge and desire to give into those emotions no matter how right it may feel. People today love to brag about cursing someone out, or showing displays of toughness, or bravado. But these are not fruits of the spirit, rather fruits of the flesh. Getting your emotions in check is at the elementary level of God's development plan for us. Many people have not advanced in their service with God or goals in life because they have not gotten past the basic fruits of the spirit that Paul speaks of.

These basic fruits have nothing to do with the commandments of God. For no one will ever be perfect and we will always miss the mark with the commandments, because every person has their individual sin they will have to constantly conquer in life. The basic fruits of the spirit are different than the commandments. These fruits of the spirit are what Paul expected the early followers of

Yeshua to have right away immediately following conversion and belief in Yeshua. Joy, love, peace, patience, kindness, goodness, faithfulness, gentleness, and self-control. These characteristics are about personality and character, rather than a decision to sin. We should possess these characteristics because of our belief in The Father and Son and the fruit of this belief comes from the Holy Spirit that will dwell inside of us.

Simeon and Levi did not surrender to these fruits, but rather the fruits that come from our sinful nature, which makes us unfit to receive our Fathers blessing, just as Simeon and Levi were unfit to receive their father's blessing.

"When you follow the desires of your sinful nature, the results are very clear: sexual immorality, impurity, lustful pleasures, idolatry, sorcery, hostility, quarreling, jealousy, outbursts of anger, selfish ambition, dissension, division, envy, drunkenness, wild parties, and other sins like these. Let me tell you again, as I have before, that

anyone living that sort of life will not inherit the Kingdom of God. But the Holy Spirit produces this kind of fruit in our lives: love, joy, peace, patience, kindness, goodness, faithfulness, gentleness, and self-control. "*Galatians 5:19-23*

We are able to effectively combat the spirit of anger if we choose to operate in the spirit of Forgiveness. Remember that Yeshua died for our sins, and that we **all** have been **guilty** of following the desires of our sinful nature. But our **new joy** rests and dwells in the promise that God has forgiven us of our sins, despite the fact that many of us can check off everything on the list of lifestyle choices that accompany the sinful nature.

God knows we are guilty of it all but he loves us enough to forgive us. **So who are we to be petty**? Who are we to not let anyone escape our wrath? Yeshua teaches we must "forgive so we can be forgiven". In the same way, spare your wrath and anger on others so that God will spare you from His wrath and anger. *"The tape we use to measure others will be the same tape God uses to measures*

us. Our words will either acquit or condemn us."
These are lessons from Yeshua. Always think of
these things before giving leeway for anger to direct
your steps.

Reflection Questions:

How does your family, friends, coworkers, view the
way you manage anger? Do they all have the same
opinion?

Have any decisions you made out of anger
redirected your paths in life?

Has your anger been the source of problems in
relationships? Has it ruined relationships?

FINAL PHASE: ARRIVING IN THE PROMISED LAND AND THRIVING IN THE PROMISED LAND

"The reality is God will fight your battles, all you have to do is show up to war wearing faith as your armor. This armor comes in the form of being the light. Light is the dress code for God's soldiers."

CHAPTER 13: THE SECRET: GOD IS WAITING ON YOU TO STEP INTO THE LIGHT

"God is light, and there is no darkness in him at all. So we are lying if we say we have fellowship with God but go on living in spiritual darkness; we are not practicing the truth. ⁷ But if we are living in the light, as God is in the light, then we have fellowship with each other, and the blood of Jesus, his Son, cleanses us from all sin." 1 John: 1:5-7

"He guided them during the day with a pillar of cloud, and he provided light at night with a pillar of fire. This allowed them to travel by day or by night. - Exodus 13*

The wilderness is not just about being tested, but it is our opportunity to observe the Lord and imitate him, so we can think like him and be like him when it is time to step into our purpose. It was in the wilderness where the Lord provided a pillar of cloud by day and the same pillar was fire by night to lead the Israelites to the Promise Land. This pillar was their compass. Anywhere the pillar went the Israelites also went. When the pillar stopped, they stopped. This was the role and purpose for the pillar of cloud and fire. The cloud was essentially there to be a compass, and the Israelites personal GPS system. Moving away from the pillar resulted in moving without God. Moses requested that the pillar always be present in order for the people of Israel and outsiders to know that God was with them and they were his people.

"If you don't personally go with us, don't make us leave this place. How will anyone know that you look favorably on me and on your people—if you don't go with us? For your presence among us sets your people and me apart from all other people on the earth." - Exodus 33: 15-16

"And the LORD did not remove the pillar of cloud or pillar of fire from its place in front of the people." Exodus 13:22

Notice that the Lord never removed the pillar of cloud from in front of his people. And He never will remove the pillar of cloud from in front of his people. The Lord was the Israelites travel guide and confirmation that He was with them. The pillar is still present today, but it is our job to be that pillar, to walk with the Lord and become the travel guide for those looking to seek His Kingdom. God's ultimate goal was for Israel to represent Him on earth as his children, and his special people.

The pillar of cloud represented the Lord and his presence in the wilderness, and outside the wilderness it will be our job to represent the Lord and be that pillar of cloud for everyone to see the light, especially those in darkness.

Learning to be the light is essential. There are several forms of light, and we have to be molded and go through the process of becoming light in the specific forms that God has called us to be as individuals. What I mean is that the moon and the sun both act as light but with the same purpose at different times. In the same way, the stars are light, but obtain a different form than the sun and moon.

God has crafted us to be unique individuals with specific forms, gifts, and callings but just like the moon, sun, and stars of the heavens we all share the same responsibility. We are made in his image to do what he would do and reflect him on earth in our specific callings as light for each other and the world. God created the sun, moon, and stars in order for us to see. Without these lights we would have no vision, and we would have no sense of direction. We would be lost.

For this reason, the mission of Yeshua was to bring sight to the blind and show those that believe they can see that they are blind. Our mission has to be the same as the Yeshua's, we need to provide direction and vision for those spiritually blind and those that believe they can see or have direction. There is no sight outside of The Messiah and God's word.

If you truly want God's purpose over your life you must reflect him. You can receive many promotions and work for many people. But until you become the light you will not work for God. He will leave you in the wilderness or in bondage until you are willing to follow his pillar of light and become one with that pillar.

"No one lights a lamp and then covers it with a bowl or hides it under a bed. A lamp is placed on a stand, where its light can be seen by all who enter

the house. For all that is secret will eventually be brought into the open, and everything that is concealed will be brought to light and made known to all.

[18] "So pay attention to how you hear. To those who listen to my teaching, more understanding will be given. But for those who are not listening, even what they think they understand will be taken away from them."Luke 8:16-18

Yeshua tells us that we are to be a light. Specifically, a candle, which indicates that we will be living around and inside of the darkness. God is omnipotent, and all-seeing. He is well aware of the darkness in this world, for this physical world belongs to God but is ruled by Satan. The Lord wants to make you a candle for the world. God will elevate you to the highest hill possible, the brighter you choose to become and according to the calling he put over your life. He needs his children to be seen, but only when we are fit for service.

To increase your light, you need to increase your proximity to Yeshua and His Father through his Word, as it is already God's plan to increase his proximity to you. Remember it is your responsibility to knock on God's door. Only then will he answer you. But ask yourself, have you sought out God's house, His Temple? This has nothing to do with your church attendance because Yeshua clearly replaces the Old Temple of Israel and all physical temples.

"Destroy this temple, and in three days I will raise it up." –John 2:19

Yeshua is the temple and you need to knock on his door. Yeshua knew God's temple in Israel would be destroyed; one of his many duties was to replace it. For the temple of Israel was where forgiveness took place, sacrificial ceremony and communication with God. Yeshua prophesied and told people ahead of time that the physical temple would be destroyed. But he dared his enemies to try and destroy him. It is your responsibility to knock on the doors of this Temple and in doing so, seek forgiveness and begin your relationship with God so that you can become the light and be as bright as he needs you to be.

"You are the light of the world—like a city on a hilltop that cannot be hidden. No one lights a lamp and then puts it under a basket. Instead, a lamp is placed on a stand, where it gives light to everyone in the house. [16] In the same way, let your good deeds shine out for all to see, so that everyone will praise your heavenly Father."
Matthew 5:14-15

God wants you to be the lamp that is made visible for the world. He wants to put you in a position on a hill for you to be seen. But it isn't for your own personal glory. It is for you to be the pillar of light by night and day for others. Your responsibility will be the same responsibility as the cloud that traveled with Israelites. You will be the guide and direction for the world when God uses you. When you become the light you become the personal GPS system for those around you.

The reason why you haven't known your purpose, haven't reached your goals, your full potential and are not being used is because YOU ARE NOT YET THE LIGHT. Light and darkness cannot be one.

One responsibility of the light is shine in darkness in order for what lies in the darkness to be made visible. This means repentance. This is not about perfection, just repentance. What lies in the dark is seen by light. Friends, family, associates, and even strangers that live lives of darkness will automatically know the blemishes within their darkness due to your light.

When you are not able to see the darkness in those who are darkness it proves you are not yet the light. You know that a flashlight is working, only if it illuminates the dark. The flashlight automatically gives light and it is made clear without dispute in the darkness.

When you are light, you naturally become a mirror for those living in darkness. The blemishes that those in darkness have will be made known because a mirror reflects. YOU WILL MAKE PEOPLE VERY FRUSTRATED! At least those that don't want to enter the light. You will be the very reminder of the bondage to sin that those in darkness choose to live in. More importantly than other people being frustrated by your light, YOU WILL MAKE *YOURSELF* VERY FRUSTRATED! Because even when you choose or try to step in the darkness you will be aware that the light is not present. You will have to leave your new self, to take part in the bondage of your old self.

In Exodus, the Lord's pillar of cloud was evident even while the Israelites were in Egypt. The plagues that affected Egypt did not affect the Israelites; the cloud was visible distinguishing that God was with the Israelites and not the Egyptians. The cloud was only with His Children, His possession. When you become the light, some people in darkness won't like you, they will hate you. You will be the evidence that God is with you and not them and that you belong to the Lord, and they don't. This is a very sad, tragic but true reality.

"The LORD said to Moses, "Lift your hand toward heaven, and the land of Egypt will be covered with a darkness so thick you can feel it." [22] So Moses lifted his hand to the sky, and a deep darkness covered the entire land of Egypt for three days. [23] During all that time the people could not see each other, and no one moved. <u>But there was light as usual where the people of Israel lived.</u>" Exodus 21-23

On the bright side, no pun intended, it is the light that will lead people to God. That is why many foreigners left Egypt to enter the wilderness with Israel and live in the Promise Land. These were the foreigners that were willing to drop their gods and worship Yahweh and live in a new land, all because they chose to follow the cloud and be a part of the light, so that they too could be included in God's possessions and property.

In the same way, you will become the light that causes those living in bondage and those who are not currently God's children to seek adoption into his everlasting family. Making sure you are the light is critical. Do not deceive yourself into thinking you are light while still being in darkness. Become the light and be seen.

"In the beginning the Word already existed.
  The Word was with God,
  and the Word was God.
He existed in the beginning with God.
God created everything through him,
  and nothing was created except through him.
The Word gave life to everything that was created,[a]
  and his life brought light to everyone.
The light shines in the darkness,
  and the darkness can never extinguish it." John 1

Reflection questions:

If people were to follow you today, where would you be leading them?

Do you direct people to the Kingdom of God?

If someone else had your vision, what would they see?

CHAPTER 14: CLOSING WORDS: LEARN TO ADAPT

" ...Much of the delay and long journey for our goals is because of failure to adapt"

When making the transition from bondage into the wilderness we will be going "cold turkey" from the cycle of work. Eat. Sleep. Repeat. All of the sudden we will have to adapt to the new change. Nothing we do for the Lord is in vain or without purpose of the bigger picture. We have to get used to changing "all of the sudden". Choosing to change "all of the sudden" is what prepares us for God's biggest picture and the most important moment in our lives.

Too often pastors teach and modern believers use the phrase "God is working on me" or

"I am a work in progress". Yes, these phrases contain truth, but take caution and understand that God frequently demands *instant change* from his people. The Israelites inability to adapt to change in their wilderness always led to complaining, which always led to sin, and delay to the promise land. So much of the delay and long journey for our goals is because of **failure to adapt**.

"I affirm, by the boasting in you which I have in Yeshua the Messiah, I die daily… For some do not have the knowledge of God, I speak this to your shame." Foolish ones for what you sow is not made alive until it dies." Corinthians 15

Do not deceive yourself into thinking you are a new person if you are still the same. Dying to the old you gives birth to the new you. This death to the old you must take place voluntarily, just as Yeshua's death was voluntary.

"I am the good shepherd. The good shepherd sacrifices his life for the sheep.[12] A hired hand will run when he sees a wolf coming. He will abandon

the sheep because they don't belong to him and he isn't their shepherd.... "The Father loves me because I sacrifice my life so I may take it back again.[18] No one can take my life from me. I sacrifice it voluntarily. For I have the authority to lay it down when I want to and also to take it up again. For this is what my Father has commanded." –John 10

The ability to adapt to these new demands, and adapt quickly will prevent your wilderness from being 40 years. Adapting to Gods' demands and commands will prepare you for the much larger picture that Paul is writing about in Corinthians. Paul is trying to prepare people to be saved eternally and preparing people for the last days.

"There are also bodies in the heavens and bodies on the earth. The glory of the heavenly bodies is different from the glory of the earthly bodies.....The sun has one kind of glory, while the moon and stars each have another kind. And even the stars differ from each other in their glory....

For just as there are natural bodies, there are also spiritual bodies….. *Earthly people are like the earthly man, and heavenly people are like the heavenly man. 49 Just as we are now like the earthly man, we will someday be like the heavenly man….What I am saying, dear brothers and sisters, is that our physical bodies cannot inherit the Kingdom of God. These dying bodies cannot inherit what will last forever…* **But let me reveal to you a wonderful secret. We will not all die, but we will all be transformed! 52 It will happen in a moment, in the <u>blink of an eye</u>, when the last trumpet is blown.** *"- Apostle Paul Corinthians 15:35-52*

Paul is preparing us for the Grand Finale, God's biggest picture for our lives. And like Paul, I am trying to get you to look forward to this transformation that will take place saving you from the wrath of God and Day of the Lord that takes place on the last day.

Now whether you want to call this moment "the rapture", the disappearing", "the vanishing", or "the transformation" is irrelevant to me. And whether you believe this happens before, during, or after THE GREAT TRIBULATION or time of testing of testing is even more irrelevant. But understand and believe that this moment will happen. And Paul says it will happen *"in the twinkling of an eye"*.

This is why that *all of the sudden change* I speak of is so critical. The reality is many aspects of our walk with God cannot be a work in progress. But they need to happen all of the sudden. Remember Zaccaheus who I spoke of in the chapter about satisfaction, and compare him with the other rich man who did not inherit eternal life. Zaccaheus was willing, able and believed in Yeshua enough to make an "all of the sudden change" in his lifestyle. There are tons of self-claiming Christians, believers, and converts who have not made the decision to die daily, and who have failed to adapt.

Be instantly changed now in order to be instantly changed later. Do not deceive yourself by thinking you are in the group of people that will be instantly changed when the last trumpet sounds, if you do not practice being instantly changed before the trumpet goes off. You have to die daily as Paul did. Make a practice of instantly changing what God requires and he will perfect that change when it's all said and done. Take everything one day at a time. Paul doesn't say he died weekly, monthly, or yearly but **daily**. Don't be intimidated by the demands of God, remember all you have to do is show up and believe. God will do the rest.

"The things which are impossible with men are possible with God."

The words of Yeshua Luke 18:27

IN LOVING MEMORY OF

KELSIE NEAL JONES

MAY 26, 1960-SEPTEMBER 29,2015